NOT JUST A MOM

NOT JUST A MOM

THE EXTRAORDINARY WORTH OF

MOTHERHOOD AND HOMEMAKING

By Lisa Anderson

Carpenter's Son Publishing

Lifeline Ministries
PO Box 8071
Spokane, WA 99203

www.lifeline-ministries.org
info@lifeline-ministries.org

Cover design by Sarah Mejia
Photography by Misty Bedwell

Published by Carpenter's Son Publishing, Franklin, Tennessee

Unless otherwise indicated, all Scripture quotations are taken from the New American Standard Bible, © 1960, 1962, 1963, 1968, 1971, 1972, 1973, Creation House, Inc.

Scripture quotations noted ESV are taken from The Holy Bible, English Standard Version (ESV), copyright ©2001 by Crossway Bibles, a publishing ministry of Good News Publishers. Used by permission. All rights reserved.

Scripture quotations noted NIV are taken from the New International Version, ©1978, Zondervan Bible Publishers.

Scripture quotations noted KJB are taken from the King James Bible.

Scripture quotations noted TMB are taken from The Message Bible, ©1993, 1994, 1995, 1996, 2000, 2001, 2002. Used by permission of Nav-Press Publishing Group.

ISBN 978-0-9828642-2-7

Printed in the United States of America.

Dedication

I dedicate this book to my mom, Ruth Makkonen Liimatta,
who was always there for me.

Acknowledgements

Many thanks are due to my wonderful friend and editor, Peggy Simpson. Because of her expertise, patience, and diligence, you are reading a much more polished book than the one I originally put into her hands.

I am grateful for DeeAnn McCuen, Janet Fish, and Patty Hardebeck. Your friendship and "like hearts" are an encouragement and strength to me.

I couldn't be the mother and homemaker I am without the love and support of my amazing husband, Jim. You live what you preach when you tell men to love their wives as Christ loved the church. Thank you for your love and care for our children and me. You are an exemplary example of a godly husband and father.

To each of our wonderful children: Thank you for showing so much grace to an imperfect mother who, like you, is on a journey of transformation with Jesus.

Where there is no vision, the people perish.

(Proverbs 29:18 KJB)

They will rebuild the ancient ruins,
They will raise up the former devastations,
And they will repair the ruined cities,
The desolations of many generations.

(Isaiah 61:4)

Contents

Chapter 1

WITH LOVE
Seek 1st
His Kingdom
+ righteousness
and His Kingdom
+ righteousness
will be given
to you.

Sense of Humor

*The truth is that years ago, before this generation
of mothers was even born, our society decided where
children rank in the list of important things. When
abortion was legalized, we wrote it into law. Children
rank way below college. Below world travel, for sure.
Below the ability to go out at night at your leisure.
Below honing your body at the gym…Children are the
last thing you should ever spend your time doing.[1]* —
Rachel Jankovic

God's sense of humor displayed itself in a big way when He placed His call on my life. *Are All Those Children Yours?*, my first book, gave credence to the blessing of children. Now, *Not Just a Mom* gives fresh vision for motherhood and homemaking. So, where's the humor? To begin with, I don't even like children—or, at least I didn't in the beginning. And, when I met the Lord as an 18-year-old college freshman and then married Jim at the age of 22, motherhood and homemaking were not even on the list of potentially important things I might do for God.

I could almost picture God looking down from heaven and asking, "Who might champion My message of motherhood and homemaking?" Perhaps many qualified young women were offered as likely candidates. But, rejecting those suggestions, I think God may have said, "No, I have a better idea. Lisa would be a perfect choice. She possesses no natural love for children and lacks vision for motherhood and homemaking. When she fulfills My call on her life, she will not be able to do it in her own strength or ability, nor will she be able to take glory or honor for herself. In fact, the message she carries will be a testimony to My grace and mercy in her life." So, humorous or not, God chose me to bear children and carry His message of motherhood and homemaking.

Scripture asks, *If the foundations are destroyed, what can the righteous do* (Psalm 11:3)? We would all have to agree that the foundational building block of society—the family—is under severe attack and, in many ways, has been destroyed. So, what are the righteous to do? If we never speak about God's ideals for family, marriage, motherhood, and fatherhood, because we risk offending people or further wounding the broken, we have no hope of reformation and will continue our slide into destruction. Therefore, it is critical we reclaim God's true purpose and design for each of these areas. In this book I will examine God's true design for motherhood and homemaking with the understanding that it is a necessary part of the reformation we need.

We live in the fair city of Spokane, Washington, home of the annual Lilac Festival each May. Every year, young women are chosen from the area high schools to vie for the position of Lilac Festival Queen. Recently, the *Spokesman Review* featured the 14 finalists who had been selected to compete for this year's title. Along with their photos, a short paragraph profiled each young lady's higher education plans, career goals, and interests. Of these contestants, two wished to become pharmacists, two were pursuing nursing degrees, four were interested in various business degrees, and one each desired to become a dentist, physical therapist, child psychologist, chemical engineer, U.S. attorney, and cosmetologist.[2] As respectable as these career goals are, I find it interesting that not one contestant declared she wanted to become a full-time mother and homemaker. Why is this?

In an age where students in seventh and eighth grade are encouraged to start making college and career plans, motherhood and homemaking are most likely at the bottom of the list of desirable career goals for women, if they appear at all. In fact, few young women are courageous enough to admit in front of peers that they want to be a full-time mother and homemaker. Most would view this vocation as a waste of one's life.

Even in the church, we tend to look "out there" for our calling instead of to the home as a valid place of ministry. A young mother bemoans this issue in the following excerpt:

> *"I wish your eyes would light up like that when you talk about becoming a mom."*
> My husband's words were piercing. We had been discussing a potential future in overseas missions, and the prospect of being a world-changer

for Jesus had become more exciting to me than the baby already in my womb.

Like many young Christians, I grew up in a church culture that emphasized foreign missions and certain exciting aspects of the Christian life. Today's church presents a lively and passion-filled message to youth, encouraging them to serve around the world and take up vocational ministries…"To the nations!" is their battle cry.

Yet, as young, married Christians seeking God's will one step at a time, my husband and I found ourselves announcing, "We're pregnant!" instead of "We're moving to Africa!" My son was born when I was 19, and we remained involved in our church and faithfully attended a weekly college-age small group. However, since the church structure did not organically integrate our lives with people outside our age group, we sort of fell through the cracks. No one brought us a meal when our son was born, and we almost felt

like we had to fend for ourselves
as we figured out marriage and
parenting.

I couldn't help but wonder what
the church's support would have
been like if we were serving
overseas instead of beginning to
raise a family at home. It seemed
like loving missions and quoting
theologians was cool, but starting
families and feeding babies was
not.[3]

But, there are exceptions. Kandice is a young woman
who, upon hearing God's truth, has come to value motherhood
and homemaking. She now looks forward to the day when she
can become a mom and homemaker. Sharing this dream with
others, however, has resulted in some incredulous responses.
When she told her dentist she wanted to be a homemaker
and have lots of children, the woman burst out laughing and
exclaimed, "I've never heard that before!"

Kandice has received similar responses from her peers
in church. As she visited a Los Angeles church, she was asked
what her future plans were. Upon sharing those plans, two
women leaders were flabbergasted and said they knew of no
one who would have the courage to admit such dreams aloud.

**I'm here to boldly declare that
motherhood and homemaking are**

**valid career choices fully worth our
time, attention, energy, and talents as
women.**

Through the years, I've come to view these as callings that
change the world, influence history, and impact the Kingdom
of God. Someone could pay me a million dollars to do anything
else with my life, but I would not accept it.

For the past 30-plus years, I've been a full-time mother
and homemaker. Am I unfulfilled? Am I bored? Have I wasted
my abilities and talents? Do I have regrets? No! No! No! And No!
In fact, I have fulfilled a vital and much-needed calling to society
and the church. I have rarely been bored. I have developed and
used my talents and abilities to serve my family, church, and our
ministry. I have been available to meet the needs of my husband
and children. And ultimately, because of this, I know I've been
part of the answer to the healing and reformation our nation so
desperately needs. On my deathbed, I will have no regrets about
my life's focus.

I want to accomplish two things in this book. First, I
want to encourage women who have already decided to give
themselves to motherhood and homemaking. Some of you are
already envisioned. If that is the case, I encourage you on your
journey. In the midst of that decision, though, some of you may
struggle with discouragement or lack of vision. The good news
is that if God can do the miracle He has done in me, then He
can do it in you, too. If you struggle with loving your children
and seeing them as gifts from God, He can give you His love for
your children and help you see them as the blessing they are.

If you lack vision for your calling as a mother and
homemaker, God can enlighten you to know that the place you

occupy is very strategic. When that place is vacated for something else, the family suffers—no matter what the "experts" say. And, when the family suffers, society and the church also suffer. Mothers and homemakers who faithfully stay at their posts and fulfill their God-given responsibilities have a hugely significant impact on the strength and health of the church and nation. With confidence, I can say that motherhood and homemaking are two of the most important contributions a woman can make to society.

Second, I want to speak to young women who are making decisions about their futures. I affirm those of you who are brave enough to publicly proclaim that motherhood and homemaking are valid career choices worth pursuing. I also want to encourage young women to wisely choose their educational and career paths. Make choices that will allow you to work from home so you can be with your children. Choose an educational path that will not burden you with such considerable debt that you are forced to work outside the home.

I also want to say a word to single mothers—a group who are walking a very hard path. Some of you are there because of poor choices made in the past, choices from which God is now healing and restoring you. Or, you may be in the unimagined position of single motherhood due to the sin and actions of others. I understand that you have the very hard job of parenting and managing a household on your own. As you read this book, it will not be difficult to see that I believe strongly in the value of mothers being home with their children. But, I know that is not possible for most of you. God is very clear in His Word that He is a Father to the fatherless and that He has a compassionate heart for the widow. And, He has asked us to carry His heart for them. Therefore, single mom, I am with you in your labors to see your family, and countless other families, healed and restored. In your attempts to meet all the varied needs of your family, may God bless the work of your hands and meet your children's needs, especially those you cannot possibly meet on your own.

The remaining chapters share truth and revelation which have inspired and strengthened me for the long-term job of motherhood and homemaking. My prayer is that they accomplish the same thing for you.

Questions for personal use or group discussion:

1. Did you feel a natural call to motherhood and homemaking? Explain.

2. Have you ever been embarrassed to admit that you are (or want to be) a mother and homemaker? Why or why not?

3. What responses have you received when you tell others that you are (or want to be) a mother and homemaker? How did those responses affect you?

4. Do you think motherhood and homemaking are undervalued in our culture? Explain.

5. If you are a mother, have you struggled with discouragement and lack of vision? Explain.

6. Do you think motherhood and homemaking are a waste of a woman's time, ability, education, and talents? Why or why not?

7. Evaluate and discuss the following quote: *The truth is that years ago, before this generation of mothers was even born, our society decided where children rank in the list of important things.*

When abortion was legalized, we wrote it into law. Children rank way below college. Below world travel, for sure. Below the ability to go out at night at your leisure. Below honing your body at the gym…Children are the last thing you should ever spend your time doing.

Chapter 2

Being There

The question here is not whether you are representing the Gospel, it is how you are representing it. Have you given your life to your children resentfully? Do you tally everything you do for them like a loan shark tallies debts? Or do you give them life the way God gave it to us—freely?[4]
—Rachel Jankovic

"Mom, I'm home!" I yelled, as I burst through the door, ready to tell her my exciting news from another day in fourth grade. "Mom? Mom?" I yelled a little louder, my voice cracking with concern. Mom was *always* there when I got home from school. So, where was she?

"I'm here," she finally responded from an upstairs bedroom where she was ironing. "I just wanted to see what you'd do if you thought I wasn't home." With a sigh of relief, I ran upstairs to pour out the news about my day.

Mom has always been there for me. She was always there when I got home from school. Plus, she was there when I walked the two short blocks home from grade school so we could eat lunch together as a family. She drove me to innumerable piano and swimming lessons and volunteered to drive our cheerleading squad to out-of-town basketball and football games. Even after I married she has always been there for me—for family moves and for the birth of each of our eight children. Sometimes I think it's easier for me to trust that God will be there for me than it is for others simply because my mom has always been there for me.

John 14:3 is a wonderful verse: "*And if I go and prepare a place for you, I will come again, and receive you to Myself; that where I am, there you may be also.*" Obviously, Jesus was talking about heaven. But, the Holy Spirit showed me that this verse is also a beautiful picture of what it means to be a mom. We get to actually be *with* Jesus in heaven! He didn't go to prepare a place for us and then leave a note on the counter saying, "I hope you enjoy your accommodations. Call if you need Me." No! Heaven is wonderful because He is there, and we get to be with Him! The Lord showed me that we mothers are privileged to provide the very same thing—our presence—for our families. In the Lord's Prayer, Jesus says to pray thus: "*Your kingdom come, Your will be done on earth as it is in heaven*" (Matthew 6:10, ESV). Our job is to bring heaven to earth. And, there is no better place to start doing this than in our homes.

Our homes should become like a little bit of

**heaven on earth, and I believe a big
part of this
is a mother's presence.**

Our local newspaper portrayed a beautiful illustration of a mother's presence as part of a series called "Life in the Hood." In the article, Tom Perko and Dee McGonigle reminisced about their growing-up-years in the Comstock Park area of Spokane. Both remembered their fathers working long hours while their mothers did double-duty at home. I love this quote from one of the men: "The mothers deserve a ton of credit," McGonigle said. "They managed the chaos and provided endless love for us. We would go over, and Mrs. Perko would be making sandwiches and just make six more."[5] Note that the moms were *present*. They managed the chaos. They provided endless love. And, they made sandwiches—lots of them—for hungry sons and their friends. While this may not sound as important as the work of a doctor, lawyer, or CEO, it is, perhaps, much more important than we realize.

Most of our friends are now empty-nesters and have been for quite some time. However, because we have eight children and our last child was born when I was 42, I still have four at home even though I am currently in my mid-fifties. And, contrary to what the media says, my presence at home is still needed and valued by my children.

In fact, the necessity of my "being there" was humorously proven one night as I tried to carve out time to work on this very chapter. Within a short time, I was approached to do the following: edit my East-coast daughter's composition for a writing contest; temporarily watch grandson Peter as Allison led a Bible study in our home; drive my youngest son James downtown to meet with friends; and finally, to have a rare phone conversation with Luke, my oldest son, about his life and music opportunities. The irritation at so many interruptions quickly turned to laughter as I realized that I couldn't say, "No," to any of those moments, especially while writing a chapter on being there for my children!

**I don't care how old our kids are—
they still need me to be
there for them as they go through life.**

Since our kitchen is headquarters-central, my children will invariably find me there when they come in the back door. My first question is always a variation of, "How did it go?" or "Where have you been?" or "How are you doing?" I know their need to share about their day is not much different than what I needed as a fourth-grader, sharing with my own mom so many years ago.

I've been blessed to realize the impact of a mom's presence in a home many times through the years. As one example, a young woman recently came to visit our home. She later shared that she started to cry while walking through the back door into our kitchen. What provoked the tears? This woman realized: *This is a real home!* She cried because she had not known this kind of home growing up.

My girls have noticed similar feelings when traveling with Jim on ministry trips. Through the years, as they've stayed in various homes, the difference between a house and a home is very apparent to them. Just as God's presence is the crucial factor in heaven being a wonderful place, I believe a mom's presence is what makes a house a home. Granite countertops, expensive furniture, and exquisite artwork offer no comparison whatsoever to a mom's presence.

Let me share another story illustrating this truth:

> While serving the poor in Calcutta, Mother Teresa once found a young boy on the streets and brought him back to Shishu Bhavan—one of the homes she established for impoverished and disabled children. There, the boy was given food and clothes—but he ran away! The next day, again the boy was brought back to Bhavan, and again he ran away. Three times the boy ran away, until on the fourth day, one of the Sisters followed him.

> "Why do you keep running away from home?" the Sister asked. The boy pointed to a tree, under which a woman was cooking a simple meal of food she had found in the garbage.

> "But this is home," he said. "This is where my mother is."[6]

Many years ago at a leadership retreat, the guest speaker was asked to prophetically minister to each of us. I waited expectantly for my turn, and when the speaker got to me, she simply said, "I see you as a large tree of peace." That was it! Then she moved on to the next woman. Honestly, I was very disappointed. How disheartening to be likened to a tree! I have since repented to the Lord for my response that day. And, to the contrary, I've come to value that word and what it represents. Just as my prophetic word likened me to a tree, Scripture likens God's people to trees. *On both sides of the river, there will grow all kinds of trees for food…Their fruit will be for food, and their leaves for healing* (Ezekiel 47:12, ESV). *Then the angel showed me the river of the water of life…also, on either side of the river, the tree of life with its twelve kinds of fruit, yielding its fruit each month. The leaves of the tree were for the healing of the nations* (Revelation 22:1-2, ESV).

We are blessed to live in an older, established neighborhood on the South Hill of Spokane, one that is covered with beautiful tree-lined streets. It is such a delight to observe the unique beauty of the trees each season. The brilliant colors of fall leaves are often breathtaking. In winter, I walk in a literal winter-wonderland as the bare branches of every tree are completely covered with icy snow. After this, there is the joy of spring buds producing beautiful flowers. And, last but not least, the mature leaf-covered branches provide welcome shade during our hot, dry summers.

In creating trees, God knew we would love shady places where our weary bodies could sit and rest. Life without the beauty and shade provided by trees would be very inferior, indeed. Trees also bless us with an abundance of fruits, nuts, flavorings and spices (cinnamon, cocoa, allspice, bay leaves, cloves), drinks (root beer from sassafras roots and tea from Camellia sinensis leaves), and some drugs (aspirin and quinine).[7]

The list goes on. In addition to providing wood for homes, trees also give shelter to numerous insects, birds, and animals. They fuel fires that are, in some nations, the only source for cooking food and providing heat. And, they "are literally our planet's lungs, constantly removing greenhouse gases from the air and producing oxygen for us to breathe."[8] "Trees can't take credit for all the oxygen in the world...Without trees, however, the air we all depend on would be rather thin."[9]

> **Beauty and delight. Shade, rest, and refreshment.**
> **Nourishment, sustenance, and healing. Shelter and warmth. Life-giving air. Those sound very similar to the things a mom is called on to provide for her family.**

A world without trees would be very different than the one we know and enjoy. And, so too, a world devoid of a mother's and homemaker's valuable contributions would be a very different and compromised life. Or, as quoted above, life devoid of a mother's presence would be rather "thin."

Some years ago, we were privileged to host a weekend visit from Sergey, the founder of Exodus Ministries in Russia. God rescued Sergey from a life of crime, drugs, and alcohol and led him to start a ministry of rescue for those with backgrounds similar to his own. He arrived at our house in December, shortly after Christmas. Snow covered the ground outside as Sergey spent several days resting with us. Wearing Jim's borrowed, fluffy sheepskin slippers, he and Jim visited in front of our living room fireplace for hours on end. Our home was festooned with thousands of twinkling white lights covering the fireplace mantles, stairwell, cupboard tops, and, of course, our eight-foot tree. It was magical.

Near the end of his visit, Sergey exclaimed in his broken English, "This like Disney!" I don't know if he had ever been to Disneyland, but I immediately knew what he meant. Disneyland is a place of delight to the senses—a fairytale kind of place where we can forget about normal life and give ourselves to happiness and enjoyment. In the midst of a hard life and wearying ministry, Sergey was saying that his time in our home was a Disneyland-type of experience—a welcomed oasis. The beauty and peace deeply ministered to his heart. Sergey (who has since gone to be with the Lord) sat under my "tree" for those few days in December and found rest and refreshment. I am bold enough to believe that the ministry he received while with us transferred, in some small way, a measure of healing to the nation of Russia.

We need to recognize the importance of being trees of healing, provision, and rest to those around us. And, by the way, the world could also use a whole lot more "chaos managers" and "sandwich makers," just like Mrs. McGonigle and Mrs. Perko in the Comstock neighborhood. Those boys could have survived without the help of these women. But, the presence and loving actions of the moms made life richer and more memorable for every one of them. Moms and homemakers catapult life from a bare existence to a rich and full experience worth living.

Questions for personal use or group discussion:

1. Was your mom there for you when you were growing up? Explain.

2. Do you think the author was correct in likening our homes and a mom's presence with heaven and Jesus' presence? Why or why not?

3. Are there women in your past who were like Mrs. McGonigle and Mrs. Perko? What role did they play in your life?

4. At what age do you think our children quit needing us to be there for them? Explain.

5. Of all the things a mom provides for her family—rest, refreshment, beauty, sustenance, a listening ear, etc.— which do you think are the most important? Why?

6. How did this chapter impact your thinking about your role as a mother and homemaker? Explain.

7. Evaluate and discuss the following quote: *The question here is not whether you are representing the Gospel, it is how you are representing it. Have you given your life to your children resentfully? Do you tally everything you do for them like a loan shark tallies debts? Or do you give them life the way God gave it to us—freely?*

Chapter 3

Confusion and War

If you grew up in this culture, it is very hard to get a biblical perspective on motherhood, to think like a free Christian woman about your life and your children. How much have we listened to partial truths and half-lies?[10] --Rachel Jankovic

Today there seems to be great confusion concerning the role of women in society. Note the ambivalence about roles expressed by this young woman in writing to Miss Manners:

> I am 23-years-old, just graduated college, and have a full-time job at a great company. I also have a boyfriend. He is truly a wonderful person with a good heart.

However, recently during an extensive conversation, he told me the following: "Sometimes I feel like the success of your career will be more important to you than your relationships. I'm not saying I want a housewife in 30 years, but I just don't want my kids' mother jet-setting around the country, missing out on their lives."

I was hurt because he brought up my grand ideas, saying that although a lot of them are exciting, he didn't know if my plans allowed room for him in my life. Honestly, at the end of the day, family, love, and friends trump all. But, I certainly deserve the right to dream and the right for those dreams to come true.

Do I need to "choose" between being the modern woman or accepting traditionalism? How do I even figure out which it is that I want to be? If it's a mix of both, how do I find the balance?[11]

Many women are asking these same questions, a reflection of an age-old war that some today call the "mommy wars." "This term refers to disputes between working moms and stay-at-home moms over one group's decision to continue to pursue a career and the other group's decision to quit work and focus solely on raising a family and running a household."12 This is not something new. I believe this is part of the war that originated clear back in the beginning of time.

When Adam and Eve sinned in the Garden by disobeying God and eating the forbidden fruit offered by the serpent, a curse was released upon each of them. The woman was cursed in childbearing, which we will see later is her primary calling. God spoke this to the serpent: "And I will put enmity between you and the woman, and between your seed and her seed; He shall bruise you on the head, and you shall bruise him on the heel" (Genesis 3:15). Enmity, according to Webster, is "hatred and the quality of being an enemy." There you have it. That is where the war between the serpent and the woman and her seed began. One way this war manifests itself is by confusion over the roles of women and the value of children.

God's original design for men and women was perfect. Sin marred all that. According to Scripture, *The creation waits in eager expectation for the sons of God to be revealed* (Romans 8:19 NIV). "The expression *eager expectation* is interesting as it pictures a man standing and waiting for something to happen, craning his head forward."13 In other words, the world is eagerly waiting for God's people to reclaim their original purpose, thereby manifesting, among other things true manhood, true womanhood, true fatherhood, and true motherhood.

As we attempt to recapture our true calling as women, we are doing so in the midst of a war and in opposition to an enemy. A big part of the enemy's

**strategy is identical to the one he used
in the Garden of Eden—falsehood and
deception.**

Allow me to share a brief history lesson that will help us understand how falsehood and deception have gotten us into the predicament in which we find ourselves today.

In 1975, Bill Bright (the founder of Campus Crusade for Christ) and Loren Cunningham (the founder of Youth with a Mission) met for lunch in Colorado. God had simultaneously given each of these men a message to give to each other. Unbeknownst to them, at the very same time, Francis Schaeffer (whose ideas helped spark the rise of the Christian Right in the United States) was given a similar message. What was it? If we are to impact any nation for Jesus Christ, we have to affect the seven mountains or pillars of society. These seven are religion, family, education, media, arts and entertainment, government, and business. Each of these leaders was called to train a new generation of change-agents to scale these mountains.14 All three men were obedient to this call.

As God is cultivating change-agents to impact cultures and nations, His enemy is also hard at work attempting to accomplish the same goal. Because of my passion, I know I am at odds with much of the feminist agenda and what it has done to demean and devalue motherhood and homemaking. So, I wanted to learn more about the feminist leaders who affected society. Who were these women? What did they believe, and why did they force their personal beliefs onto the culture? My conclusions were both educational and eye-opening.

Susan B. Anthony and Elizabeth Cady Stanton were two of the most influential suffragettes; they dedicated their lives to winning the right to vote for women. Both women did their work in the 1800s, a period when females had few rights and little opportunity. Husbands had absolute control over their wives financially, sexually, and in every other way. Women had no economic rights—so much so, that even the money they earned belonged to their husbands. Women could receive no formal education. In cases of divorce, husbands were always given custody of the children. Alcoholism was rampant, and many women found themselves married to drunk, controlling, and abusive husbands. Anthony and Stanton, along with many other women, fought long and hard to reverse these wrongs, believing if women got the "vote" they would have power to secure their rights and rise out of oppression. So, who were these two change-agents, and what did they believe?

Anthony was raised a Quaker, grew up in a very activist family, and worked for the abolition of slavery in addition to fighting for women's rights. However, she never married. She once said, "No true woman could sacrifice herself for the love of one man and wind her life around his whims, instead of developing her own life and talents."[15] Anthony became known as "America's most celebrated proponent of a woman's right to remain single and completely independent of men."[16] While I can applaud some of Anthony's work, I find no Scriptural grounds for her views on marriage, men, or the foundation of womanhood. I don't believe she is the ideal woman for whom we are searching.

Elizabeth Cady Stanton wrote this: "Nothing that has ever emanated from the brain of man is too sacred to be revised and corrected…Now the time has come to amend and modify the prayer books, liturgies, and Bibles…women's imperative duty at this hour is to demand a thorough revision of creeds and codes, Scriptures, and constitutions."[17] She went on to write *The Women's Bible*, reinterpreting Scripture from a feminist viewpoint. Rebelling against all tradition of the era, Stanton struck the word *obey* from her wedding vows and refused to be called Mrs. Henry Stanton, insisting on being known as Elizabeth Cady Stanton.[18] She once had the privilege of hearing Charles Finney speak. (Finney was the famous revivalist of the 1800s through whom one million souls were reportedly saved.) Yet, instead of being convicted by God's truth, Finney's preaching actually terrorized Stanton for months, and she decided to follow a more rationalistic, scientific worldview.[19] Again, Stanton's desire to help women was commendable, but I would not point to her accomplishments and worldviews as worthy of following.

Another influential feminist change-agent was Margaret Sanger, founder of Planned Parenthood. She published the feminist magazine *The Women Rebel* with the motto: "No God, No Masters." Its first issue in March 1914 denounced marriage, property laws favoring men, established religion, capitalism, and laws against contraceptive information. "A woman's duty," Sanger wrote, "was to look the world in the face with a go-to-hell look in the eyes…to speak and act in defiance of convention."[20] She was clearly an anti-Biblical change-agent opposed to God's truth and ways. Tragically, her greatest legacy, Planned Parenthood, is an organization that has become one of the largest abortion and contraceptive providers and promoters in today's world.

Betty Friedan, another feminist crusader, was the author of the wildly popular book *The Feminine Mystique*. Her book propelled hundreds of thousands of women to leave their homes and enter the workforce. It ignited the contemporary women's movement in 1963 and, as a result, permanently transformed the social fabric of the United States and countries around the world. She eagerly signed the Humanist Manifesto II[21] which declared: "No deity will save us; we must save ourselves."[22] In 1966, Friedan helped found the National Organization for Women, serving as its first president. In 1969, she was a founder of the National Association for the Repeal of Abortion Laws, now known as NARAL Pro-Choice America.[23]

Friedan is yet another example of a woman who hated God and used her life and influence to promote ungodly values in society. Unfortunately, her influence on culture has been profound. According to Benjamin Wiker in *10 Books that Screwed up the World*, "Friedan wanted both a happy home and, at the same time, freedom from its constraints to pursue what she considered to be more valuable and meaningful activities. Perhaps this is her most dangerous legacy. She helped spawn the notion that a combination of a very part-time motherhood with a full-time professional life was an achievable and desirable goal. Against almost all psychological research, she argued that children would feel loved if mothers gave them a kiss in the morning and a kiss at night and left them to schools, day cares, and televisions in between."[24]

These culture-changers rightly diagnosed some of the problems of women in society and correctly highlighted the need to remedy those problems. Tragically, in their reactionary and anti-God stances, they offered the wrong answers—answers that have been very detrimental to the family and society. Scripture says, *"Beware of the false prophets...you will know them by their fruits"* (Matthew 7:15-16). If you examine the fruit of these notable feminists' lives, it is not difficult to see that their fruit has been very poisonous and destructive indeed.

As prominent culture-changers, it would behoove us to further examine these women's beliefs—beliefs that have become entrenched in the culture and have had a profound effect on women and the choices they make today. What false ideals did they believe and promote?

- ❧ All three feminists viewed marriage, children, and homemaking as oppressive callings which kept women from personal fulfillment and establishing a productive place in society.

Friedan wrote: "We can no longer ignore that voice within women that says, 'I want something more than my husband and my children and my home.'"[25] "Many women feel frustrated and are apart from the great issues and stirring debate for which their education has given them understanding and relish. Once they wrote poetry. Now it's the laundry list. Once they discussed art and philosophy until late in the night. Now they are so tired they fall asleep as soon as the dishes are finished. There is often a sense of contraction, of closing horizons and lost opportunities. They had hoped to play their part in the crises of the age, but what they do is wash the diapers."[26] "A profession or job outside the home was what every woman now needed."[27]

- ❧ All three strongly rejected the idea that "biology is destiny." In other words, they believed that women could not reach their full potential if they limited themselves to childbearing and homemaking.

Friedan wrote: "Abortion had to be confronted. You couldn't have woman's equality without her own control of the reproductive process. The time when biology was destiny and women's lives were defined mainly by their reproductive function was over as far as the women's movement was concerned. The personhood of women required the emergence from passivity, biology, and men's laws."[28]

🙠 Betty Friedan also proposed that abortion and childcare were essential issues if women were to take their rightful place in the world. She said, "Women needed complete control over their reproductive lives if they were to become fully emancipated."[29] She also proclaimed that "without childcare, it (the feminist movement) is all just talk."[30]

I will further examine these topics in the following pages through the lens of God's Word. Before I do that, though, let's look at the lives of several women who have lived the false dream these feminist leaders so ardently promoted. If the fruit of their lives is good, then we should fully embrace their beliefs. However, if the fruit has been destructive, then we need to reject their teachings and determine how their false views may have affected our own lives and choices.

Questions for personal use or group discussion:

1. What is your view of the "good old days" in terms of motherhood and homemaking?
2. Do you think we have already seen a good model of womanhood in history? Or, do you agree with the author that we are still waiting for God's ideal to reappear? Explain.
3. In what ways was the author's history lesson of the feminist change-agents and their beliefs eye-opening to you?

4. Do you agree with the feminists that the answer to the problems women face is abortion and childcare? Why or why not?

5. All three feminists viewed marriage, children, and homemaking as oppressive. They believed these things kept women from personal fulfillment and establishing a productive place in society. Do you agree or disagree? Why?

6. What do you think of Friedan's notion that a combination of part-time motherhood and full-time professional life is an achievable and desirable goal for women? Explain.

Chapter 4

A Broken Model

---

*Women, who now constitute a critical mass in the
workplace, have learned through
exhaustion, divorce, and disappointed children that
trying to fit their lives into the male mold
of success was like trying to squeeze into Cinderella's
shoe.[31]* –Kathleen Parker

You've come a long way, baby! was the 1960s slogan for Virginia Slim cigarettes. Obviously, women have come a long way. Many have attained high positions on the mountains of influence. Female judges, doctors, lawyers, CEOs, and heads-of-state are commonplace today—nothing is beyond our reach. However, in our quest for equality with men, I believe we've lost sight of our God-designed role as women. In attaining high positions of power and influence, many women have made huge personal sacrifices in the process—sacrifices that are very costly indeed.

Let's examine some of these sacrifices paid for "progress" and the resulting consequences to society.

Rosie the Riveter was the popular symbol of World War II women who filled industrial positions traditionally held by men in society, spots that were vacated when thousands of men left to fight the war. Rosie's proud image was a muscular, flexed bicep, symbolizing a strong woman who could do anything a man could do. Her willingness to sacrifice for her country in a time of need was commendable. Unfortunately, Rosie's presence in the work world meant she was now absent a good part of the time from her traditional place in the home. This absence had some serious consequences according to an article entitled "The American Family in World War II."

> Although the war had opened up new opportunities, it also brought much sadness and a far more serious reality regarding life in its normal state. Separation from fathers or sons left devastating effects, and in a sense, many (children) felt robbed of their childhood. With the family shifting roles, each member was initially shocked and filled with mixed emotions. With added stresses it was an emotional time, to say the least—the American family would undoubtedly be changed forever. Those factors contributed to an upsurge in divorce, resulting in severe problems among the

young. There were five million "war widows" trying to care for their children alone. Women employed outside the home left tens of thousands of "latchkey" children who were unsupervised much of the day. The rates of juvenile delinquency, venereal disease, and truancy rose dramatically. The impact on the family was evident, attended by much anxiety about the breakdown of social values.[32]

Rosie and the thousands of women she represented materialized during a national crisis. Life was not normal in America. To come to the aid of our nation at war, women left their homes to take over men's work in society. Out of the home, though, many women found it hard to return once they tasted a new "liberation."

Please understand that I am not against the liberation of women. We all have greatly benefited from women's progress in society and the equal status we now enjoy.

However, when our new accomplishments affect the foundation and health of the family, and ultimately the foundation and health of the church and nation, we need to evaluate our priorities very carefully.

The Lord convicted me one day with this thought: *Just because we can do anything a man can do, doesn't mean we should.* In other words, just because we are free to leave our place in the home and do the work a man does, does not mean that it is always in our best interest or the best interest of our children, family, or society to do so. *Washington Times* columnist Jonetta Barras states it this way: "Women have ventured so far away from a woman's geography and into the foreign terrain of men that we have lost ourselves. We have forgotten the habits, expressions, and values that made us different but not less equal to men. The lawlessness of our children, the destruction of our communities, and the escalation of the divorce rate lend credibility to the charge that our wanderings have been devastating."[33]

Natalie Massenet is a very successful businesswoman who built a $76 million business by offering high-end fashion with overnight delivery straight to the home. How did she accomplish this? One of her keys to being a successful female entrepreneur was simple: "Choose the right nanny and choose the right husband."[34] So, someone else raised her children as she influenced the mountain of business. That's a price I'm unwilling to pay.

Let's take a closer look at what Massenet's lifestyle might entail by examining the life of another female high-achiever. Anne-Marie Slaughter was the first woman director of policy planning at the State Department, a foreign-policy dream-job. Following is a portion of her story as told in the *Atlantic Monthly*:

> I found myself in New York, at the United Nations' annual assemblage of every foreign minister and head-of-state in the world. On a

Wednesday evening, the President and his wife hosted a glamorous reception at the American Museum of Natural History. I sipped champagne, greeted foreign dignitaries, and mingled.

But, I could not stop thinking about my 14-year-old son, who had started eighth grade three weeks earlier and was already resuming what had become his pattern of skipping homework, disrupting classes, failing math, and tuning out any adult who tried to reach him.

Over the summer, we had barely spoken to each other—or, more accurately, he had barely spoken to me. And, the previous spring I had received several urgent phone calls—invariably on the day of an important meeting—that required me to take the first train from Washington, D.C., where I worked, back to Princeton, New Jersey, where he lived. My husband, who has always done everything possible to support my career, took care of him and his 12-year-old brother during the week; outside of those

midweek emergencies, I came
home only on weekends.[35]

Slaughter went on to share that she soon left her government job and returned home to scale back on her workload. In her words, "Juggling high-level government work with the needs of two teenage boys was not possible."[36] We need the refreshing honesty of women like her to reinforce the truth that when women work outside of the home, this choice has serious ramifications for the family. In fact, as Slaughter discovered, she couldn't successfully do both at the same time.

Golda Meir was prime minister of Israel in 1969 during a pivotal time in her nation's history. Many point to her as an example of a successful female head-of-state. But, what most people don't know is that early on in her career Meir had an abortion, feeling at the time that her political career could not accommodate a child.[37] At a later point, she realized she could not fully give herself to her family and her career and after careful consideration, chose her political career over her family. Meir worked hard at her new career, but always felt guilty about not doing enough to save her marriage. She also felt guilty about neglecting her children.[38] While Meir would never have called herself a feminist, author Sandee Barwarsky, in her book *Golda Revisited*, said things differently: "She (Meir) was my kind of feminist, like, 'Get out of my way and let me do what I want, and could you please get over my gender?'"[39] She wasn't going to let gender stand in her way. Since Meir's reign as prime minister, many men and women have chosen as she did, but many have also suffered serious regrets over these choices later in life.

Margaret Thatcher served England as prime minister from 1979-1990. She, too, could be held up as a powerful and

successful model of a woman in government. However, few stop
to consider that she reportedly had a rocky, tenuous relationship
with her adult children.[40] I believe no amount of worldly acclaim
is worth the risk of jeopardizing a close, loving relationship with
my children or husband. To sacrifice those relationships is much
too high a price to pay for success of any kind, as far as I am
concerned.

The new-found freedom of women has many
ramifications. In the article "Does Greater Equality Mean Less
Happiness?" author Katherine Kersten suggests that women's
contentment might possibly be found in the traditional roles
they have rejected. She quotes a Wharton study entitled "The
Paradox of Declining Female Happiness" which reports that
women's sense of well-being has declined, in spite of their
equality with men.

> Why this flip-flop on happiness
> by the most fortunate generation
> of women in history? Why have
> progress and liberation on every
> front—educational, professional,
> and sexual—left many women in
> a funk?...What does seem certain
> is that the path to liberation and
> expanded opportunity has entailed
> some unsettling tradeoffs.
>
> Take the sexual revolution. In 1970,
> women on my college campus
> began sporting T-shirts declaring,
> "A woman without a man is like a

fish without a bicycle." In their eyes, marriage and family were a ball and chain—more likely to bring women bondage than fulfillment. To find happiness and an authentic identity, they insisted, women would have to cast off social convention and obligations to others and "explore" their sexuality without restraint.

But this philosophy had a catch: men began to embrace it too. Encouraged by women, many men began to back away from the responsibilities and burdens of marriage and fatherhood and to join enthusiastically in the sexual free-for-all. Increasingly, they came to view women as sex objects—the very thing feminists had claimed to want to avoid—rather than as long-term partners in the common enterprise of family.

We know what followed: Marriage and family began to unravel. The divorce rate doubled between the mid-1960s and mid-1970s. Today, no one of either sex can count on marriage or family for the social support we need to get through life's inevitable challenges. But women and children—more vulnerable—have paid the biggest price.

Women's quest for happiness in the work world also brought tradeoffs. In the 1970s and '80s, many women, long shut out from high-powered careers, confidently sought freedom and fulfillment from a shiny briefcase and a VP nameplate on the office door. Success brought financial self-sufficiency and a fuller stage for the use of talents.

But the search for identity in the work world also brought disappointment. As women pinned their hopes for happiness on professional careers, they began to discover the mixed bag their male counterparts knew too well: the pressure to produce, the outright drudgery, the risk of failure, the boss from hell. For some, the process may have shed light on why men have traditionally died at a younger age.

Maybe we women got the whole happiness thing backwards. Years ago, we assured ourselves of a golden road ahead if we could throw off all that had tied us down and limited our options in the past. But perhaps there was something in those ties themselves—those "prisons" of family, marriage and other fundamental obligations—that had the power to bring us closer to our true goal.[41]

Dr. James Dobson founded Focus on the Family in 1977 when he became increasingly concerned about the breakdown of the traditional family and its negative effect on the culture. I value his long-term perspective and understanding. When asked what one factor has done more damage to families than any other, Dr. Dobson had this to say:

It would be the almost universal condition of fatigue and time pressure, which leaves every member of the family exhausted and harried. Many of them have nothing left to invest in their marriages or in the nurturing of children. Fifty-nine percent of boys and girls come home to empty houses every afternoon, during which time anything can happen.

This hurried lifestyle also puts great pressure on women. Many of them are trapped in a chaotic world that constantly threatens to overwhelm them. Some of these young women grew up in busy, dysfunctional, career-oriented households, and they want something better for their kids. Yet, financial pressure and the expectations of others keep them on a treadmill that renders them unable to cope.

I have never said publicly what I will share now—and I will be criticized for saying so in this context—but I believe the two-career family *during the child rearing years* creates a level of stress that is tearing people apart.

And it often deprives children of something they will search for the rest of their lives.

If a scale-back from this lifestyle, which I call "routine panic," ever grows into a movement, it will portend wonderfully for the family. It should result in fewer divorces and more domestic harmony. Children will regain the status they deserve, and their welfare will be enhanced on a thousand fronts. We haven't begun to approach these goals yet, but I pray that a significant segment of the population will awaken someday from the nightmare of over-commitment and say, "The way we live is crazy. There has to be a better way than this to raise our kids. We will make the financial sacrifices necessary to slow the pace of living."[42]

As I mentioned earlier, just because a woman is educated and capable of successfully filling any position open to her does not mean that that is always her best course of action—especially if she still has children at home. Contrary to what the world may say, our greatest place of influence in society and the greatest mark we could make for eternity could very well rest in our position as mothers and homemakers who carry God's heart.

What does *God* say on the matter? What is *His* original intent for us as women? I will explore this in the next chapter.

Questions for personal use or group discussion:

1. Do you agree with the author that, in our quest for equality with men, we've lost sight of our God-designed role as women? Explain your answer.

2. Explain your thoughts about the following statement: *Just because we can do anything a man can do, doesn't mean we always should.*

3. Evaluate and discuss the following: *Women have ventured so far away from a woman's geography and into the foreign terrain of men that we have lost ourselves. We have forgotten the habits, expressions, and values that made us different but not less equal to men.*

4. How do you feel about the family sacrifices the following women paid for their success on the mountains of business and government—Natalie Massenet, Anne-Marie Slaughter, Golda Meir, and Margaret Thatcher? Do you feel their success was worth the price they paid?

5. Dr. Dobson said the following: "I believe the two-career family *during the child rearing years* creates a level of stress that is tearing people apart. And it often deprives children of something they will search for the rest of their lives." Do you agree or disagree with his statement? Why or why not?

6. Evaluate and discuss the following quote: *Women, who now constitute a critical mass in the workplace, have learned through exhaustion, divorce, and disappointed children that trying to fit their lives into the male mold of success was like trying to squeeze into Cinderella's shoe.*

Chapter 5

Our Great, Great, Great, Great Grandmother

---

*Women aren't happy precisely because they tried
to fit themselves neatly into the male template of
what constitutes happiness…men and women are
different.[43]* –Kathleen Parker

We come from a long line of mothers. Our great, great, great, great (back more generations than I care to count) grandmother's name was Eve. Three chapters into the Bible, Genesis says, *Now the man called his wife's name Eve, because she was the mother of all the living* (Genesis 3:20). Eve had the wonderful distinction of being the very first woman and the very first mother. Scholars follow certain laws of biblical study when they study Scripture. The Law of First Mention states that there is great significance to something when it is mentioned in the Bible for the first time. The fact that the first woman was called a mother is significant throughout the remainder of Scripture whenever women are mentioned. Additionally, it holds great meaning for our lives today, many generations later.

> **As much as some people want to separate women from the role of motherhood, it is clear that, from the beginning, God equated women with motherhood.**

We've already read that outspoken feminist Betty Friedan declared that women needed to avail themselves of abortion and childcare to take their rightful place in the world. In other words, she believed women needed to separate themselves from motherhood and children in order to become fully liberated. These both contradict God's original design for us as women.

Feminists take great issue with the idea that "biology is destiny"—that our destiny is determined by our God-given design. It is easy to determine the purpose of something by its design. Obviously, men were not created to bear and nurture children because they lack the needed anatomy. As women, though, God gave us wombs and breasts for the purpose of bearing and nurturing children. Not only does the first woman speak of this, but so does the very design of our physical bodies. I love the insight Bob and Jan Hess give this in their book *Full Quiver*. They know of no other healthy, functioning body system we attempt to stop or thwart other than our reproductive system.[44] In our human wisdom, we try to temporarily or permanently stop the ability to reproduce (have children) in order to follow some other more seemingly important calling or destiny. We seem to believe that biology does, indeed, hinder our destiny. But, this premise is faulty and unbiblical.

As we further examine womanhood, it is highly significant that the curse on Adam and Eve, because of their sin, also gave credence to our God-given design. The man was cursed in his work, and the woman was cursed in childbearing. *To the woman He said, "I will greatly multiply your pain in childbirth; in pain you shall bring forth children."...Then to Adam He said..."Cursed is the ground because of you; in toil you shall eat of it all the days of your life."* (Genesis 3:16-17). The English Standard Version study notes on this verse state that "this curse of pain at childbearing strikes at the very heart of the woman's distinctiveness, for she is the mother of all the living."[45]

If only the male calling was valuable, God would have stopped with the creation of man. However, in making human beings in His image, God chose to make both men and women—two distinct beings who individually and together display His glory and image. When women abandon or reject their God-given design to become like men and pursue their calling, something is lost of the reflection of God's image and glory. Something is also lost of His purposes in the earth.

Contrary to the world's viewpoint, God's unique design and calling on our lives as women is vital and not to be abandoned as we search for our full potential.

We have already discovered that our physical design and the curse of sin speak to us about motherhood. So, what else does Scripture have to say about the purpose of women? The apostle Paul, in his instructions to the church, addressed the issue of caring for widows in the community. He observed that many younger widows emerged as gossips and busybodies. As a result, Paul gave the following instructions: *Therefore, I want younger widows to get married, bear children, keep house, and give the enemy no occasion for reproach* (1 Timothy 5:14). In other words, he was exhorting widows to forsake the life of a busybody and gossip and get back to their main calling of motherhood and homemaking.

The young widows whom Paul was addressing were exhorted to do the very same thing that God told Adam to do. *Then the Lord God took the man and put him into the Garden of Eden to cultivate it and keep it* (Genesis 2:15). Young widows were told to "keep house," and Adam was told to "keep the garden." So, what does *keeping* entail?

To keep house means: "the master of the house, exercising authority." It also means: "to govern or manage a household."[46] These are words of leadership: master, authority, govern, and manage. The enemy has convinced us that a mother and homemaker is a woman of no influence. *Au contraire!* It is a position of God-given authority and responsibility. The home is the place on earth we have been given dominion of as women.

Webster's definitions of *keep* are rich and serve to greatly expand the understanding of our calling: "to retain in one's power or possession; not to lose or part with; to have in custody for security or preservation; to preserve from falling or danger; to protect, guard, and sustain; to keep in order; to supply with the necessities of life." Keeping house goes far beyond the physical care of our homes—washing dishes, doing laundry, preparing meals, etc. Our job covers so much more than that. We are called to retain our home and family in our power or possession, not letting the enemy gain control over them. We are commissioned to keep our children secure and protect them from danger. And, while keeping our homes in order, we are also to supply our family with the necessities of life. Wow! That is quite a job description!

What else does Scripture say to us about our calling? *Older women…encourage the young women to love their husbands, to love their children, to be sensible, pure, workers at home, kind, being subject to their own husbands, that the Word of God may not be dishonored* (Titus 2:3-5). The duty to be workers at home doesn't mean that women can't do other things. However, this passage of Scripture indicates that our first priority, especially as younger women, should be to our husbands, homes, and families.

Titus tells older women to encourage younger women to be workers at home. That could easily sound like a life of menial labor. However, according to Webster, *work*, too, is a word loaded with rich meaning: "to form by labor; to mold or shape; to manage or lead; to produce by action, labor, or exertion; to direct the movements of." Again, these are all action words of leadership: form, mold, manage, lead, shape, and direct.

> **Webster's definition of *mother* is also significant: "the matter from which all things are made." In other words, mothers are the source of all life. Who we are and what we do is hugely significant.**

Feminists would have us believe that being a mother and homemaker entails a life of menial labor and drudgery, squelched dreams, unfulfilled passions, and unutilized abilities. But, according to the above portions of Scripture, our calling is a rich and valuable one. Women are not second-class citizens because they have been given a different calling than men. God, in His love and wisdom, has given women a sphere of influence that is essential to the good of mankind. I believe we have it within our capacity as mothers and homemakers to mold and shape not only the lives of our children, but also society at large.

These revelations about the worth and value of being a keeper-of-the-home radically changed my life. Scripture says, *Where there is no vision, the people perish* (Proverbs 29:18 KJB). This is exactly what happens to women who don't have a vision about their calling as mothers and homemakers. They can't see past the sinks of dirty dishes, piles of laundry, dirty diapers, and snotty noses. They can't see a light at the end of the tunnel. But, when we think God's thoughts about our calling, it gives vision and purpose to everything we do.

I believe God intends the home to be the center of society from which all of life radiates. The home used to be the center of education, benevolence and care for the poor, hospitality, religious training, and commerce. Now we look to government to provide many of those things for us. We expect the government to educate our children, care for the poor, take care of us, and meet all our needs. As a result, home has become the center of almost nothing. For many, home is just a place to shower and sleep. I believe God wants us to reclaim the home for all it was intended to be. Armed with God's truth, we can become vital, fruitful women, and our homes can become busy hives of Kingdom activity.

Questions for personal use or group discussion:

1. What are your thoughts on "original design" as seen in the life of Eve? Do you think it is a valid description applying to all women? Explain your answer.

2. Do you think the idea that "biology is destiny" is limiting to women and something we need to be freed from? Why or why not?

3. Did the definitions and interpretations of keep, work, and mother change the way you think about the role of mothers and homemakers? Explain.

4. Do you agree or disagree with the feminist viewpoint that motherhood and homemaking prevent women from living up to their full potential? Why or why not?

5. Have you lacked vision for motherhood and homemaking? If so, how has this affected you?

6. Evaluate and discuss the following quote: Women aren't happy precisely because they tried to fit themselves neatly into the male template of what constitutes happiness…men and women are different.

Chapter 6

Unsung Heroes

> *Live the Gospel in the things that no one sees.*
> *Sacrifice for your children in places that only they will*
> *know about. Put their value ahead of yours...Your*
> *testimony to the Gospel in the little details of your*
> *life is more valuable to them than you can imagine.*
> *If you tell them the Gospel, but live to yourself, they*
> *will never believe it. Give your life for theirs every day,*
> *joyfully.*[47]   –Rachel Jankovic

During a recent prayer mission to Washington D.C., our group visited the Tomb of the Unknown Soldier. We saw the changing of the guard and were privileged to observe the retirement of one of the honor guards who had completed his two-year assignment. The Tomb of the Unknowns is a monument dedicated to American service members who have died without their remains being identified. On the west panel of the monument is this inscription: *Here rests in honored glory an American soldier known but to God.*

It is a great privilege to be chosen as a guard for this tomb, and few attain the honor. The soldiers must commit two years of their lives to guard the tomb. They live in barracks under the tomb and cannot drink any alcohol (on or off duty) or swear in public for the rest of their lives. For the first six months of duty, a guard cannot talk to anyone, nor watch television. All off-duty time is spent studying the 175 notable people laid to rest in Arlington National Cemetery. Every guard spends five hours a day getting his uniforms ready for guard duty. As he walks back and forth across the tomb, the soldier on duty takes 21 steps in one direction and then turns and takes 21 steps in the other direction. This corresponds to the 21-gun salute—the highest honor given any military or foreign dignitary.[48] The extent of their sacrifice is astonishing and gives honor to unknown heroes who gave their lives for our country.

In today's world, honor is usually given to those with important titles or lots of money. Mothers and homemakers cannot boast of these things. Most of our job is hidden; people never see what we do. Even the Proverbs 31 woman received accolades solely from her husband and children, not great crowds of people.

Following is an honest reflection from a mother of four. She describes well the struggles of dealing with a lack of recognition and honor as a mom:

> Comparison is an ugly thing. 2 Corinthians 10:12 tell us that it is not wise to compare ourselves with others. (Sigh)…That is so

true. It's hard being a mom when other people say things about their busyness, and I can tell they derive value from their accomplishments outside the home. It's also difficult when single women are not very impressed with my life and rarely see me doing anything they consider valuable.

It's challenging seeing working moms with stylish clothes and professionally groomed nails and hair, while my big shopping day entails hitting thrift stores. I admit I have even been envious of people in ministry sharing about the people they mentor. I am mentoring my four children, and no one is grateful or impressed when I teach them something new.

On the other hand, I am so glad I'm around my kids and get to spend intimate times talking with them and hearing their hearts. I get the opportunity to gently correct their subtle thoughts of self- righteousness or insecure feelings that wouldn't be noticed if I wasn't with them day-in and day-out. My budding teenager's words, "Everyone my age has had a boyfriend but me," can be talked about openly as I impart peace to her heart about the whole subject of relationships. Today I taught my kids about heaven and worshiping God in everything we do. I visibly saw them grow closer to the Lord and be filled with hopeful joy and imagination of our heavenly future. Those things are worth so much more than fancy clothes and manicured nails!

I wouldn't trade the decision we made for me to stay home and raise our kids for all the outside affirmation in the world. My children will only be young for a short time (Well, when they were toddlers, it seemed like an eternity!) and as they grow into adulthood, I know I will not regret my priorities.

We need to remember that, just like the unknown soldiers buried at Arlington Cemetery, we are known by God. He sees and knows our labors. He sees and knows the work of our

hands done in secret, away from the
public eye.

He sees every diaper we change, every meal we fix, and every load of laundry we do. He sees us awake in the wee hours of the night with a fussy baby or sick child. He hears the prayers and groans we offer up for our children—for their salvation, safety, protection, and futures. He knows every sacrifice we make and every selfless act of love we perform for our families. And, He is pleased.

But, even in knowing this, it's easy for me to spiral down into a pit of self-pity. I remember a special church event where self-pity really tried to overtake me. I was helping at a youth conference, and in addition to housing and feeding nine out-of-town guests for two nights, I also volunteered to work at the registration table. Because our table was separated from the main conference area by a big divider and black curtain, I had little opportunity to interact with anyone besides my co-workers. Jim had been sick all week long but decided to attend on Saturday afternoon to hear our daughter speak. Many out-of-towners recognized him because he travels and ministers extensively to young people. As we entered the building, young people immediately flocked around him exclaiming, "Pastor Jim! Pastor Jim!" Simultaneously, one young woman turned and said to me, "Oh, I guess I'll hug you, too." Feeling very marginalized, I fought back tears of self-pity as we made our way down the hall.

Right then I had a choice to make. I could agree with the enemy's lies about my life, or I could believe God's truth about me. I chose to believe God's truth by rehearsing these words: *God sees me and knows my work and labor. God is pleased with the work of my hands. He has given me a very high calling. My faithfulness as a mother and homemaker contributes greatly to the health and well-being of the church and the nation. I rest in a place of God-given authority and dominion. My life, faithfully lived out, will affect history and the Kingdom of God. I am so much more than "just a mom." The assignment I have been given is one of good and blessing. It is strategic and essential.*

In the midst of feeling "hidden," it is good to realize that only a handful of people ever receive top recognition and notoriety. Even among Jesus' twelve disciples, very few, if any of us, can list all twelve by name. I could only list seven or eight the first time I tried. Of course, everyone can list the top three—Peter, James, and John. Everyone remembers the traitor Judas Iscariot. Most would recollect Matthew, the tax collector, and Andrew, Peter's brother. It is also hard to forget doubting Thomas. But how many of us can list Phillip, Bartholomew, James (son of Alpheus), Simon the Zealot, or Judas (son of James)? These men were Jesus' hand-picked disciples who turned the world upside down. It seems inconceivable we cannot list all twelve of them! How would you like to be known as the "other James" or the "other Judas"? Just as Phillip, Bartholomew, the other James, Simon, and the other Judas were often overshadowed by the other more famous disciples, we too, as mothers and homemakers, are often overshadowed by others who are in the public limelight.

DeeAnn came to my rescue one day when she relayed a dream she had about me. She told me God was very pleased with my life and the choices I had made. For ten minutes, she shared words of affirmation and blessing over me as I sat listening on the phone, tears running down my face. Even I, a veteran mother of many years, need to be reminded that God values my life and calling. I long to hear that God values the choices I have made. You, too, need to know that God values your life and the work of your hands as you care for your children, home, and family.

Even our mundane tasks carry special significance to God. One night I went to bed feeling like I had not accomplished much all day. (That is especially unsettling to someone like me who tends to value my days based on productivity and tangible results.) As I lay in bed, I decided to list what I had done in the past 24 hours. Over breakfast, I scanned the new food ads in the newspaper to see if there were any noteworthy specials. Our daughter was hosting a personal wedding shower for one of her best friends that evening, so I helped prepare the house and prayed with her that the shower would be a special blessing to all who attended. I watched James as he performed a science experiment. I helped Maggie and James figure out Christmas presents for various family members. After I made a bank deposit for our ministry, I stopped and faxed a form to the IRS. Since my parents were moving into our mother-in-law apartment in a couple of weeks, I cleaned out a few closets to make room for some necessary shifts in the household. I made sure I had tacos ready for the kids before they all left for youth group. And, last but not least, I spent the evening with a friend who is standing in faith for the restoration of her marriage. The sum total of my day was a very ordinary day in the life of a mother and homemaker.

The Holy Spirit then led me to consider the consequences if I had not carried through with the day's tasks. By ignoring the food ads, I could have missed out on some good bargains to help keep our food bill reasonable. Without my help, Molly would have felt stressed out and overwhelmed as she prepared for the shower. But, my assistance and prayers helped her and resulted in a blessed night for Tory, just days before her wedding. If I had been absent, James would have had no one to share his delight in making "plastic rock." I insured a blessed Christmas morning by planning appropriate gifts for family members. Even though Jim was currently ministering in Canada that week, my behind-the-scenes office work for the ministry was, and is, equally important to the success of our ministry. Because it is pleasing to God that we are caring for my elderly parents, my prep work for their arrival was valuable. And, I know my family is blessed every time I prepare a meal for them and meet their needs. Finally, I believe my time with my friend was a blessing to her and pleasing to God. As I was reminded of God's viewpoint, my statements became faith-filled declarations and affirmations as I evaluated my day. Instead of falling asleep dissatisfied, I went to sleep peacefully, feeling the pleasure of God.

> The thing that is so important for us to keep before us is that if we choose not to do this very special job, it will simply not get done. The mothering, nurturing, comforting, and caring that fill the committed homemaker's day will simply be lost, and society will be impoverished. Women can give up their jobs as clerks, engineers, salespeople, doctors—other people will step in and the world will go on as smoothly as before…The groceries will still be sold, trucks loaded with

merchandise will still roll across our highways, and Wall Street will carry on. Not so with homemaking. We are the special people into whose hands the homes of the country and the world have been entrusted. When we leave this job the world does *not* go on as before. It falters and begins to lose its way. We homemakers are indispensable. Homemaking is much more than a job—it is profession; a profession which is venerable, honorable, and of the highest benefit to mankind. We must not forget this.[49]

Questions for personal use or group discussion:

1. If you are a mother and homemaker, have you struggled with a lack of affirmation and value in your calling? If yes, how has this affected you? If no, how has this affected you?

2. How did the example of the Tomb of the Unknown Soldier minister to you? Is it enough for you to know that God sees and values the work of your hands?

3. What lies commonly assault you regarding your value as a mother and homemaker?

4. What truths do you (or could you) use to counteract those lies?

5. Do you agree or disagree with the statement that society is impoverished when women focus on callings other

than motherhood and homemaking? If you agree, in what ways do you believe society is impoverished? If you disagree, what are your reasons why?

6. Evaluate and discuss the following quote: *Live the Gospel in the things that no one sees. Sacrifice for your children in places that only they will know about. Put their value ahead of yours… Your testimony to the Gospel in the little details of your life is more valuable to them than you can imagine. If you tell them the Gospel, but live to yourself, they will never believe it. Give your life for theirs every day, joyfully.*

Chapter 7

The Bonbon Myth

God uses childbearing and raising, within families, to
draw women—and men—to Himself. Both women
and men learn that they are not the center of the
world—that they belong to their spouses and to God.
Self-focus is the chief obstacle to God-focus, and
when family trumps self, the road to transformation
providentially becomes open.[50] —Rachel Jankovic

With the feminist viewpoint entrenched in our society, mothers and homemakers are frequently the objects of ridicule and scorn. "Barefoot and pregnant" is a derogatory figure of speech that some use to describe mothers and homemakers. *Barefoot* signifies that a woman is at home and therefore does not need shoes. *Pregnant* is associated with being helpless and being a baby-making machine with no career or life of her own.[51]

Another demeaning quip from the past is that housewives just "sit on the couch watching soap operas and eating bonbons." (Bonbons are small sweet candies dipped in chocolate. I have never had a bonafide bonbon, but if it is dipped in dark chocolate, I am already a fan!) I emphatically deny that this is the life of a stay-at-home mother and homemaker. Most full-time homemakers I know are busy, accomplished women. I will introduce you to a few of them. But before I do that, I'd like to examine the life and activities of a godly woman from the perspective of Scripture.

So, what dos the life of a godly woman look like? She was certainly not the subjugated woman of the 1800s who had little, if any, possibilities open to her and was forced to live far below her potential. Neither was she the post-Depression-era woman who found herself with nothing meaningful to do as the growing acceptance of birth control resulted in having fewer children and the industrial revolution provided appliances to cut her work-load in half. Nor, I believe, is she the emancipated woman of the 21st century who pursues her own agenda and goals, often to the demise of marriage and family.

Proverbs 31, however, gives us a hopeful and helpful picture of a woman who faithfully meets the needs of her household, and, over a lifetime, lives a very satisfied and fulfilled life.

Who is the Proverbs 31 woman, and how did she spend her days? According to Scripture, she was not idle, but steadfastly attended to the welfare of her household. She was busy providing her family with meals and making sure they had the appropriate clothing for every season. She was always looking out for the best interests of her husband, which I'm sure included practical, spiritual, and emotional support. Her character was marked by kind speech, strength, dignity, and a positive, faith-filled vision for the future. She also met the needs of the poor and needy. And, last but not least, she purchased real estate, grew productive crops, and ran a clothing and belt business. Now, from this very full description of her life, it is unlikely this Proverbs 31 woman had any time to sit on her couch, watch soap operas, or eat bonbons!

Paul's first letter to Timothy tells us of another godly woman. Paul clarifies the qualifications a widow should have in order to receive help from the church. He states that she should be...*the wife of one man, having a reputation for good works; and if she has brought up children, if she has shown hospitality to strangers, if she has washed the saints' feet, if she has assisted those in distress, and if she has devoted herself to every good work* (I Timothy 5:9-10). Regarding these qualifications, the ESV Study Bible notes say this: "The list of qualifications provides a picture of a godly older woman, giving something for younger women to aspire to."[52] Though less comprehensive, this list closely parallels the life of the Proverbs 31 woman in that she marries, raises children, and cares for the needy.

Some would say that Proverbs 31 could justify women working outside of the home. But, there is nowhere that says she left home to conduct any business. She could have done all her work *from* her home. Quite possibly, she could be a good model of a home-based entrepreneur. And, nowhere does it claim she accomplished all of these things simultaneously or that she did them when her children were small. Proverbs 31 could easily represent a woman's entire life as lived over a number of years.

It is possible that she focused on outside activities once her children were older. I, for one, would have been overwhelmed trying to run a home-based business when I was in the midst of raising small children. Now that my children are much older, I am freer to give myself to other endeavors.

Let me introduce you to some wonderful women who are living the life of the Proverbs 31 woman. If you are a young mom raising small children (or, an older woman, for that matter), please do not let the following testimonies make you feel like you need to take on additional responsibilities if you do not feel the grace to do so.

> **I share these examples to help us see
> that a woman does not need to leave
> her home in order to use her gifts,
> follow her passions, fulfill her dreams,
> or live a meaningful life.**

I'd like to start with two of my special friends. Patty and Janet have each successfully raised four children (along with the help of their husbands, of course!). All of their children are now married and producing wonderful grandchildren whom Patty and Janet help with as much as possible. Patty has faithfully supported her husband Tom in the ministry for the last 20-plus years. Janet and James have been involved in lay-ministry for many years and own their own custom cabinetry business, for which Janet does the books. Both women are currently caring for one of their elderly parents at home. Neither one has been the CEO of a company or held public office. In fact, beyond their immediate spheres of influence, their names are unknown. But, I believe these women are very pleasing to our Heavenly

Father. Their focus continues to be biblical, based on the Scriptural examples we mentioned earlier. I know their children and husbands would rise up and praise them—just as did those of the Proverbs 31 woman. If I were to give an A-one example of a godly woman for the next generation to follow, these two women would appear right near the top of my list.

What about some examples of other women who are right in the middle of raising small children? I can think of a number of young moms who are faithfully meeting the needs of their families while simultaneously exercising their gifts and callings—right from home.

- Lisa (another Lisa!) homeschools her young daughter and works with her husband in managing their many rental homes. They have housed numerous foreign students and students from church over the years. She has used her amazing gift of administration in numerous capacities at our large and growing church. They are currently exploring the foster-to-adopt program.

- Our oldest daughter Allison is starting to homeschool her children. Until recently, she did the books for her husband's growing lawn maintenance business. She leads a small-group Bible study for young women and serves with her husband on the leadership team for our church's young adult ministry. She also has a knack for creative decorating and throws amazing, memorable parties.

- Joann homeschools her young daughter and has tutored a number of our children in math, attempting to transfer her love of math to our non-math-loving family. In addition to housing many foreign students over the years, she and her husband welcomed Terrie, a long-time friend, into their home for six years. Suffering from a life-threatening lung disease, Terrie determined she would not die, would get off oxygen, and believed in God for her future. Miraculous things happened. She received a lung transplant, discarded the oxygen, and is now married! Mike and Joann were blessed to be an active part of those miracles in Terrie's life.

§ Another homeschooling mom, Heidi, teaches her four children at home and helps teach at various homeschool cooperatives. Heidi loves to cook, develops new recipes, and has entered numerous cooking contests. She blesses special friends by serving at their wedding receptions. She also faithfully supports her husband in his ministry of coaching soccer. Recently, they started a part-time, home-based business as a family.

§ Marianne is busy raising her small children, oversees the finances for her husband's business, and assists him in heading up the missions' ministry at our church—a natural outgrowth of having been raised in China by missionary parents.

§ As head of the music ministry at our church, Jessica oversees a large group of musicians and singers, plans the Sunday worship services, and leads weekly practices. A mother of three daughters, she has also done medical billing right from her home.

- My friend Chris (we share grandchildren—her son Jesse married our daughter Allison) is an accomplished woman. She homeschooled all seven of her children and is currently the master teacher for a large homeschool cooperative. Not only does she use her education degree, she also serves as the children's pastor at their church where her husband is the senior pastor.

- Michelle, who is also raising small children, turned her love of photography into a successful, part-time wedding photography business.

- Another young mom volunteers her photography skills to photograph single moms and their newborns at the local Life Services maternity home.

- Katie turned her framing and sewing expertise into home-based businesses, bringing in extra income for her family.

- Our second daughter Bethany has done a variety of things since she married. Before they had children, she simultaneously managed a four-star restaurant and assisted her husband David in serving as youth pastors. There, she also served as a worship leader. Now, David is in law school. To bring in needed income for her family, Bethany has turned her love of thrift shopping into a profitable online business.

- Bonnie, the mother of four adorable sons, is a leader in their young adult ministry and is part of a team that facilitates their church's discipleship program.

What have I done in my 30-plus years of motherhood and homemaking? I've homeschooled all eight of our children. I've helped Jim in writing two books and am now writing this, my second book. Together we've provided housing to over twenty young people over the years—a sometimes challenging but overall rewarding experience. Administration is natural for me, and I've used my skills in our ministry and in serving at church. I have led various small groups for young moms, teaching and providing encouragement. We were privileged to care for Jim's mom in our in-law addition for two years before she passed away. And now, my own parents have moved into that apartment, and I'm blessed to assist them in this season of their lives.

I could list many more women who are meeting needs or serving society right in the middle of motherhood and homemaking. Some volunteer at the local crisis pregnancy center, others take in and care for foster children, and still others have adopted children into their families. Some are using education, training, or skills to bring in extra income for their families. Others are exercising abilities in needed volunteer work at churches or in other organizations. But, most importantly, they are building stable families and homes in the midst of a world where those things, though desperately needed, have become scarce commodities. I, right along with their husbands and children, praise their efforts.

Questions for personal use or group discussion:

1. Have you ever faced ridicule or scorn in your primary calling as a mother and homemaker? If so, how did you deal with it?

2. In the past, how have you viewed the Proverbs 31 woman? Has she inspired or intimidated you? Explain.

3. What do you think about the author's interpretation of the Proverbs 31 woman—that this chapter well describes her activities lived out over a lifetime? Does this change your perspective on her life and its application to your own life?

4. Do you agree or disagree with the author that the Proverbs 31 woman could be a good model of a home-based entrepreneur? Why or why not?

5. How do the present day examples of women's lives and activities affect you? Do they bring encouragement and vision to you? Why or why not?

6. Do you believe women can fully use their gifts and talents in the midst of motherhood and homemaking? Why or why not?

7. Evaluate and discuss the following quote: *God uses childbearing and raising, within families, to draw women—and men—to Himself. Both women and men learn that they are not the center of the world—that they belong to their spouses and to God. Self-focus is the chief obstacle to God-focus, and when family trumps self, the road to transformation providentially becomes open.*

Chapter 8

Words

When my little girl told me, "Your hands are full!"
I was so thankful that she already knew what my
answer would be. It was the same one that I always
gave, "Yes, they are—full of good things."[53]
–Rachel Jankovic

Current statistics tell us that fifty percent of pregnancies are unplanned. This means that, "Oh, no! I'm pregnant!" are the first words spoken over many children. Instead of hearing, "I'm so excited you are here!" or "You are such a gift from God!" the first words many children hear are, "I don't want you right now," or "You are a horrible mistake and will ruin my life!" In light of Proverbs 18:21 which tells us, Death and life are in the power of the tongue, these words have great power. Our words either bless and release life, or they curse and release death.

Even something as innocent as a Christmas newsletter can speak the negative. I remember reading one that greatly saddened me. The mother wrote: "One down. Two to go. Can't wait until we are empty-nesters!" Taken literally, she was telling her children, "I can't wait until you are gone!" Now, I understand many people can feel that way in light of raising challenging teenagers. I also understand that in this day of fractured marriages and families, raising children (and step-children) is not the blessed endeavor God intended it to be. And, this mother was, perhaps, tired and ready to be released from the enormous daily task of raising children. But, her words are not idle ones. They do not release blessing and life to her children. In fact, I cringe to think that her children possibly read what she wrote.

God has plenty to say about our tongues and the power of words. According to Matthew 12:34, what comes out of our mouth is a reflection of what is in the heart: *"For the mouth speaks out of that which fills the heart."*

> **Furthermore, our words not only reveal what is in our heart, they also determine our current and future realities.**

Let me explain. God prepared Moses to lead the Israelites out of bondage in Egypt and then promised to bring them to the Promised Land (Exodus 6:6-8). He demonstrated His great power by executing the ten plagues on Egypt and parting the Red Sea. On top of that, His visible presence accompanied them in a cloud by day and a pillar of fire by night. Day and night they could look and see He was with them. The Israelites should have had complete confidence in God—that

His promises were true and that He had the power to bring these promises to pass.

But, tragically, whenever the Israelites encountered need, they completely forgot God's words of promise and previous works of power. This led them to utter words of despair, unbelief, and accusation. The first time they met with hunger on the journey, they responded: *"Would that we had died by the Lord's hand in the land of Egypt, when we sat by the pots of meat, when we ate bread to the full; for you have brought us out into this wilderness to kill this whole assembly with hunger"* (Exodus 16:3). When they lacked water, they reacted in similar fashion: *"Why, now, have you brought us up from Egypt, to kill us and our children and our livestock with thirst?"* (Exodus 17:3). Far from being idle words, the Israelites determined their fate. God allowed it to happen just as they had spoken. *"Just as you have spoken in My hearing, so I will surely do to you; your corpses shall fall in this wilderness, even all your numbered men, according to your complete number from twenty years old and upward, who have grumbled against Me. Surely you shall not come into the land in which I swore to settle you"* (Numbers 14:28-30). They spoke their own death sentences. Wow! That makes you want to set a guard over your mouth!

If our tongues have so much power, what can we do to grow in our ability to speak life-giving words? *Thy word have I treasured in my heart, that I may not sin against Thee* (Psalm 119:11).

When God's Word is hidden and stored up in our heart, it increases the possibility that His Word will come out of our mouth in any and every situation.

This power of words has many applications in our lives. Years ago, God showed us His truth about children. We realized that the words so often used by society to describe children—burden, hindrance, hassle, and liability—completely contradict God's words about children—blessing, reward, and gift. God's words became such a part of our hearts that the first words over our children were always words of blessing. In fact, His words have brought unspeakable life and joy to us. We were never afraid of getting pregnant and always viewed it as a blessing. We've never felt our child-raising years to be a burden, nor are we looking forward to an empty nest so we can get on with other things. Instead, we are enjoying every last minute we can get with each of our children. They *are* the important things in life.

If the first words over your children were words of cursing instead of blessing, there is still hope for you. *If Thou, Lord, shouldst mark iniquities, O Lord, who could stand? But there is forgiveness with Thee* (Psalm 130:3-4). You can repent for believing a lie and speaking a curse over your children. If appropriate, you can even repent to your children—no matter what their age. You can explain that you did not have God's perspective when your first words over them were words of rejection. Then you can explain that God's truth has changed your heart and that you now know, beyond a shadow of a doubt, that they are a blessing and gift from Him. And, it's never too late to start speaking words of blessing over your children. Regularly say to them, "You are such a blessing to me. I am so glad you are my son (or daughter.) You are a gift from God to us." These words will release life to them.

God's words changed my life in another significant way. Earlier in life, I struggled a lot with anger. I easily got impatient and would burst out with angry words. Then we attended Bill Gothard's Institute in Basic Life Principles seminar, and he challenged all of us to memorize Romans 6 and 8—the entire chapters. He assured us it would be life-changing. I took him up on the challenge and proceeded to memorize those two chapters. As I meditated on these words: *Do you not know that when you present yourselves to someone as slaves for obedience, you are slaves of the one whom you obey, either of sin resulting in death, or of obedience resulting in righteousness?* (Romans 6:16), they began to transform my life. I realized that every time I succumbed to anger, it resulted in death to my family and me. The opposite was also true. Every time I gave myself to patience and kind words, it produced life and blessing to those around me. As a result, I no longer struggle with anger as a major issue in my life.

As we sow God's Word deep into our hearts, we experience many benefits. I declare the following benefits when I read His Word:

- *He who gives attention to the Word shall find good* (Proverbs 16:20). *Thank you, God, that good will comes to me as I am faithful to be in your Word.*

- *All Scripture is inspired by God and profitable for teaching, for reproof, for correction, for training in righteousness, that the man of God may be adequate, equipped for every good work* (2 Timothy 3:16-17). *God, use your Word today to teach and train me. Use it to bring reproof and correction into my life. Thank you that all Scripture is inspired by You (even the seemingly boring and dull parts) and is included for a reason.*

- *Like newborn babes, long for the pure milk of the Word, that by it you may grow in respect to salvation* (1 Peter 2:2). *Lord, thank you that your Word will help me grow in salvation and sanctification.*

🙌 *My son, give attention to my Word; incline your ear to my sayings. Do not let them depart from your sight; keep them in the midst of your heart. For they are life to those who find them, and health to all their whole body* (Proverbs 4:20-22). *Thank you that Your words will bring life and health to me.*

🙌 *Thy word is a lamp to my feet and a light to my path* (Psalm 119:105). *Lord, thank you that Your Word will give guidance and direction to me.*

🙌 *For the Word of God is living and active and sharper than any two-edged sword, and piercing as far as the division of soul and spirit, of both joints and marrow, and able to judge the thoughts and intentions of the heart* (Hebrews 4:12). *Lord, may Your Word be living and active in my life today.*

🙌 *How blessed is the man who does not walk in the counsel of the wicked, nor stand in the path of sinners, nor sit in the seat of scoffers. But his delight is in the law of the Lord, and in His law he meditates day and night. And he will be like a tree firmly planted by streams of water, which yields its fruit in its season, and its leaf does not wither; and in whatever he does, he prospers* (Psalm 1:1-3). *Lord, thank you that Your Word will be life-giving to me and cause me to prosper and be fruitful in every season.*

Wow! The benefits of the Word in our life are enormous: teaching, reproof, correction, and training—equipping us for every good work; spiritual growth; life;

health; guidance; refreshment; fruitfulness; and prosperity. The alternatives are also significant: ignorance, lack of correction, and lack of training—making us ill-equipped for good work; stunted spiritual growth; death; sickness; confusion and lack of direction; fruitlessness; and a lack of prosperity in the seasons of life.

> **If we want to aspire to the model of the Proverbs 31 woman—who was fruitful and prosperous in every season of life—it will only happen as the Word of God becomes the centerpiece of our lives.**

It took the Israelites 40 years to enter the Promised Land—the place where God's promises to them were finally realized. It could have happened much sooner if they'd sown His words into their hearts and then spoken them out of their mouths. The Bible tells us that every time they encountered need, it was a test from God to see how they would respond. In like fashion, all of us will be tested, too. In fact, this is a huge part of our walk of faith as believers.

The Word of the Lord promising Abraham and Sarah a son tested them for twenty-five years until their promise came to pass. In the process, God changed Abram's name to Abraham. It took considerable faith for childless Abram (meaning exalted father) to declare that his name was now Abraham (meaning father of a multitude). He had to agree with God's words over his life and begin declaring them out of his mouth. I imagine he had a lot of incredulous responses when people asked this "father of a multitude" how many children he had and he answered, "None." In faith, Abraham had to overcome his own embarrassment and the mocking of some to continue declaring God's words over his life—words which stood in stark contrast to his current reality. But, both he and Sarah learned to...*consider Him faithful who had promised* (Hebrews 11:11), and they eventually obtained their promise.

The Word of the Lord also tested Joseph in Genesis 37-46. *And He called for a famine upon the land; He broke the whole staff of bread. He sent a man before them, Joseph, who was sold as a slave. They afflicted his feet with fetters; he himself was laid in irons, until the time that His word came to pass, the Word of the Lord tested him* (Psalm 105:16-19). As a young man, Joseph dreamed twice that he would sit in a place of headship. Enroute to that promise however, he was sold into slavery by his brothers and imprisoned falsely on sexual charges. He could have easily given in to despair and become a revengeful, bitter man. Instead, I believe he held firmly to the words and vision God had given him. Interestingly, he always ended up in a place of headship—even as a slave and prisoner. Potiphar made Joseph, a slave, overseer of his house. And, the head jailer placed Joseph, even though he was a prisoner, in charge of all the other prisoners. Joseph eventually attained the place of headship over a nation—the ultimate fulfillment of God's promise to him.

Jesus was tested, too. In Matthew, we read the story of Jesus' baptism and the subsequent temptations he endured in the desert. God spoke these words over Jesus at His baptism: *"This is my beloved Son, with whom I am well pleased"* (Matthew 3:17). In the ensuing 40 days Jesus spent in the wilderness, twice the devil challenged those words: *And the tempter came and said to Him, "If you are the Son of God, command that these stones become bread"* (Matthew 4:3) and, *"If you are the Son of God, throw yourself down"*

(Matthew 4:6). I believe Jesus' time of testing was relatively short compared to that of the Israelites (40 days versus 40 years) because He firmly believed God's words to Him and did not give in to the devil's challenge of those words. Jesus knew He was God's beloved Son. Therefore, He did not need to prove anything by turning stones into bread or doing any other miracle.

In every test we encounter, we can either speak our own words of panic and unbelief, or we can speak God's words of promise, hope, and provision. The words we choose to speak have consequences. Our words either bless and release life, or they curse and release death. So, it's critical that we saturate our lives, minds, and spirits with God's Word. Taking regular time for this is one of the most beneficial decisions we can make as moms and wives. It will transform our thinking and dictate what comes out of our mouths. It will hasten our entrance into the Promised Land—the place of God's promises being fulfilled in our lives.

A young mother recently wrote a column complaining about the hardships of motherhood. Unfortunately, her negative words solicited many similar comments from other moms. Motherhood *is* hard. I felt terrified when, after the birth of my first-born, my mom drove away after helping me for a week. I had no idea how to care for a baby by myself. Cracked, bleeding, and painful nipples during my first weeks of nursing were horrible and were something no one had ever warned me about. Months of little sleep with a newborn were difficult. Numerous times I have felt inadequate and overwhelmed as a mother. However, instead of focusing on the difficult aspects of motherhood and inviting other moms to gripe and complain with us, it will be much more beneficial if we speak God's truth to ourselves and others:

❧ *Consider it a sheer gift when tests and challenges come at you from all sides. You know that under pressure, your faith-life is forced into the open and shows its true colors. So don't try to get out of anything prematurely. Let it do its work so you become mature and well-developed, not deficient in any way* (James 1:2-4, TMB). In other words, we are to let the tests and challenges of motherhood bring us to maturity and fullness of faith.

❧ *Lay aside every encumbrance, and the sin which so easily entangles us, and let us run with endurance the race that is set before us, fixing our eyes on Jesus, the author and perfecter of faith, who for the joy set before Him endured the cross* (Hebrews 12:1-2). If Jesus could endure the suffering of the cross for us, surely we, as mothers, can endure relatively minor pain and inconveniences for the joy and privilege of raising our children. This is one reason it's important for older moms to mentor and encourage younger moms. Since we've been through it, we can cheer you on and say, "You will make it. All your hard work and sacrifice is worth it for the joy and reward of raising godly children."

❧ *"If any one wishes to come after Me, let him deny himself and take up his cross, and follow Me. For whoever wishes to save his life shall lose it; but whoever loses his life for My sake shall find it"* (Matthew 16:24-25). Successful motherhood definitely requires a "losing of our lives." It requires a gracious surrender of many things that are precious to us: our time, our sleep, our attention, our own agenda, our very bodies. However, as we learn to lay down those things, we will find life—that which truly matters.

🙟 *Women shall be saved through the bearing of children* (1 Timothy 2:15). One commentary says that *saved* here means sanctified. I can testify to the fact that bearing and raising children has conformed me more to the image of Christ than anything else in my life. Quoting from my first book: "Children have saved me from a life of toxic self-absorption."[54] As much as my flesh has hated it at times, that has been a very good thing.

🙟 *But we have this treasure in earthen vessels, that the surpassing greatness of the power may be of God and not from ourselves... Therefore we do not lose heart, but though our outer man is decaying, yet our inner man is being renewed bay by day. For momentary light affliction is producing for us an eternal weight of glory far beyond all comparison* (2 Corinthians 4:7, 16-17). Again, the afflictions of motherhood are producing good fruit for eternity in our lives.

In summary, what is our best response to the hardships of motherhood? Is it to complain and invite others to complain with us? No! That will only result in death. Our best response is found in 1 Thessalonians 5: 16-18: *Rejoice always; pray without ceasing; in everything give thanks; for this is God's will for you in Christ Jesus.* We will encounter hardships in all seasons of life. My flesh is currently not enjoying the sleepless nights that accompany post-menopause and older age. However, His Word tells us: *This is the day which the Lord has made; Let us rejoice and be glad in it* (Psalm 118:24). Since we are exhorted to rejoice in the day He has made, I am also choosing to rejoice in my sleepless nights. You, too, young mom, can choose to rejoice in the challenges of motherhood that cause you to need Him more, seek Him more, and find Him more. You can also rejoice that He has given you the great privilege of partnering with Him in raising up your little ones for His glory and purposes. Not only will you make it through, but you will be changed in the process and come out looking more like Him, more conformed to the image of His Son.

Questions for personal use or group discussion:

1. In what ways did this chapter on *words* impact you?
2. What were your first words over your children? Why were you led to speak those words?
3. Do you think the author was too hard on the mother who wrote: "Can't wait until we are empty-nesters"? Why or why not?
4. What are the promises of God that you find difficult to believe for in daily life?
5. What do you think of the author's statement that when we regularly sow God's Word into our hearts, that His Word will then more readily come out of our mouths? Explain.
6. In what areas are you currently being tested? How are you handling the test? What do you think will be the sign that you have passed this particular test?
7. Discuss the following quote in terms of your past: *When my little girl told me, "Your hands are full!" I was so thankful that she already knew what my answer would be. It was the same*

one that I always gave, "Yes, they are—full of good things." Are these the types of words that were spoken over you as a child? If so, how did that affect you? If not, how did that affect you?

Chapter 9

Cheerios

Apart from Me you can do nothing (John 15:5).

Surrounded by the demands of daily life, it is often difficult to find time to spend with the Lord. I know it seems almost impossible at times for mothers of small children to carve out a quiet time in their daily schedules. In fact, legend has it that Susanna Wesley, mother of the famous revivalists John and Charles Wesley (and 17 other children!), pulled the apron over her head when she needed time alone with the Lord. This was a signal to her children not to interrupt her.

When my own children were small, I decided that my times with the Lord didn't need to be "quiet." I am not an early riser, so I was never one to get up at the crack of dawn and complete my quiet time before the kids woke up. So, instead of serving them breakfast right away, I gave them all small containers of Cheerios to stall them. Oftentimes, I would put the baby in her crib with a bowl of Cheerios. By the time I was done, there were Cheerios all over the place! But, cleanup was a small price to pay for spending time in the Word and pouring out my heart to God.

> **Now that my kids are older, they tell me it greatly impacted their lives seeing me take time with the Lord on a daily basis. I didn't have to tell them that the Lord came first in my life or that time with Him was important. I was, instead, showing them by my example that it was so.**

Even Jesus, the Son of God, regularly left the crowds who continually sought Him and went away to a quiet place to pray. I believe one of the reasons He did this was because He desperately needed God's help, wisdom, and strength. Remember that He, too, was fully human. Time with the Lord is the key to determining if we will be victorious in daily life. I don't "have to" take daily time with the Lord, but I desperately need Him in order to survive, thrive, and live an overcoming life.

As we have already discovered, the Proverbs 31 woman was quite the woman! How did she faithfully meet the needs of her family and do it with a positive, cheerful attitude? I believe the answer is found here: *She girds herself with strength and makes her arms strong* (Proverbs 31:17). Let's examine what this means.

Using Webster's 1828 Dictionary definition of *gird*, the verse could be said this way: "She clothes herself with strength."

The Proverbs 31 woman put on a very beautiful piece of clothing called strength. I'm assuming it was an essential undergarment she wore daily since strength characterized her life. It was a staple to her wardrobe. Webster tells us that *strength* means "the power by which we can move ourselves; vigor; firmness; toughness; the quality by which we can sustain the application of force without breaking or yielding; the power of resisting attacks; and a spirit of animation."

According to these definitions, when we neglect to clothe ourselves with strength, we suffer dire consequences. Without strength, we are lazy, idle, and sluggish—not equipped to do the work God has called us to do. A lack of strength makes us weak and fragile. The Bible calls us to have quiet, submissive spirits (1 Peter 3: 1-3), but we are definitely not called to be weak or fragile. On the contrary, we are to be spiritually firm and tough. Without strength, we are like Eve in the Garden, unable to resist attacks from the enemy. The demands of motherhood, homemaking, and life in general may dishearten us, discourage us, and cause us to want to quit. We might be tempted to give up on our marriage. Temptation may want us to give up on our faith or the church. Being clothed with strength enables us to resist these temptations. And finally, without strength, we lack a spirit of animation and are characterized by a deadness of spirit.

Our friend, the Proverbs 31 woman, is not meant to condemn us. Neither is she meant to hold up an impossible standard that forever shames us or makes us look bad by comparison. Instead, her purpose is to instruct and encourage us. Out of all the things she did—brings, works, looks, rises, gives, considers, buys, plants, stretches, grasps, extends, makes, supplies, and teaches—the only action directed at herself is found in verse 17: *She girds herself with strength and makes her arms strong*. She knew this was the key to her success. If it was that important to her, it would be good for us to understand what this means for our own lives.

Strength is essential if we are to succeed at motherhood and homemaking. However, strength did not automatically come to our sister in Proverbs 31, nor does it automatically come to us. When Scripture tells us she girded or clothed herself, it implies action on her part. We find King David demonstrating the very same action. 1 Samuel 30 tells the story of David and his men returning from battle and discovering that an enemy had attacked their city, burned it down, and taken their wives and children captive. David not only lost his two wives, but was greatly distressed because the people were talking of stoning him to death because of the loss of their families. In that context, Scripture tells us…*David strengthened himself in the Lord his God. Then David said to Abiathar the priest, the son of Ahimelech, "Please bring me the ephod."…And David inquired of the Lord…*(1 Samuel 30:6-8). Both David and the Proverbs 31 woman strengthened themselves in the Lord. The order in which David did this is also significant. He *first* strengthened himself in the Lord. Then, and only then, did he call for the priest.

It's a regular temptation for women to look to their husbands to meet their needs. Unfortunately, husbands were never designed to meet all of our physical, social, spiritual, or emotional needs. Nor are our leaders or girlfriends meant to be the primary source we turn to when in need. Only God is fully adequate for this task. We are to seek Him first.

Ephesians 6: 10-11 tells us: *Be strong in the Lord and in the strength of His might. Put on the full armor of God, that you may be able to stand firm against the schemes of the devil.* These verses contain two commands. The subject of every command is understood to be *you*. Thus, these commands could read: *You*, be strong in the Lord. *You*, put on the full armor of God. We are called to be women of strength, vigor, spiritual toughness, and vision. All of these take effort on our part.

Oftentimes, though, we are like my husband Jim when, as a child, he pretended to be asleep after late night family visits away from home. His parents would then have to carry him from the car to his room, undress him, and tuck him in bed. We can easily adopt that same posture. Often, we want someone to do things for us and take care of us spiritually. However, Scripture is clear that we need to clothe *ourselves* with strength.

What is the source of our strength? Obviously, it's God. *The Lord is my rock and my fortress and my deliverer, My God, my rock in whom I take refuge; My shield and the horn of my salvation, my stronghold. I call upon the Lord, who is worthy to be praised, and I am saved from my enemies* (Psalm 18:2-3). *Wait for the Lord; be strong, and let your heart take courage; yes, wait for the Lord* (Psalm 27:14). *I have learned to be content in whatever circumstances I am. I know how to get along with humble means, and I also know how to live in prosperity; in any and every circumstance I have learned the secret of being filled and going hungry, both of having abundance and suffering need. I can do all things through Him who strengthens me* (Philippians 4:11-13).

Our church begins each New Year with a 21-day fast, and we are encouraged to not only fast from something but to fast unto God. Since I am a workaholic at heart and felt the need to work on relationships, I decided to read *The Sacred Romance* by Brent Curtis and John Eldredge—a book about our relationship with God—during this year's fast. Curtis and Eldredge explain that when we seek anything else besides God to meet our needs, those sources can become our gods.

Upon contemplating that truth, I came to the realization that I usually find my satisfaction and meaning in work and productivity. When I feel dissatisfaction or soul-hunger and thirst, my normal response is to do something productive, thereby checking another project off my to-do list. During the fast, I determined, instead, to seek God every time I felt an inner thirst. The result was amazing! He satisfied me and filled me up when I sought Him in my need. To a greater degree than ever before, I learned to make God the source of my strength and satisfaction.

The things we typically turn to for satisfaction, refreshment, and strength—food, our girlfriends, time with our husbands, a shopping spree, our favorite television show, or work—none of these things will ultimately satisfy or strengthen us. Only God will.

How do we access the strength that is found in Him? The following story helps answer this question:

Fourteen years ago, when Marjorie Newlin was 72, her neighborhood supermarket had 50-pound bags of kitty litter on sale. Without anyone to help her carry the bags back to her house, she struggled mightily under the load. Never a particularly athletic woman, but staunchly independent, she decided that she had to do something about her deteriorating physical capabilities.

The elderly woman began lifting weights—for her cat. "I want to be as independent as I can be, for as long as I can," said Newlin, a great-grandmother and retired nurse…"I just want to do things for myself."

After 13 years of weight training, Newlin is more than taking care of herself. At her two-story home in Mt. Airy, Newlin runs up the stairs with the sprightliness of a 10-year-old and has a room dedicated entirely to her plaques, certificates, and trophies (some almost as tall as her) from bodybuilding competitions around the world.

"I chuckled when I saw this little old lady walk inside the gym," says Richard Brown, a personal trainer at Rivers Gym.

Newlin quickly showed him what an older athlete could do. "She kept coming in day after day, week after week, and month after month," Brown remembers. "She didn't

want to do 'girly' workouts. She
wanted to train with us fellows."[55]

How did Newlin progress from being a frail, elderly woman to a world-class champion bodybuilder? She did so by strengthening herself on a daily basis. Day after day, week after week, and month after month she went to the gym and worked out. Consistency over time made all the difference. The result? She became a strong woman—a very strong woman.

The same model holds true for us. We will not become strong women of God by occasionally taking time with Him or sporadically opening our Bibles. Nor will we be characterized by strength if we only call out to Him in times of crisis. But, as we go to Him day after day, week after week, and month after month, we will come to be characterized by His strength. Consistent saturation in His Word will transform our minds and continually remind us of His promises, power, and faithfulness. Time spent magnifying Him in worship will put our earthly problems in perspective. If those things become regular parts of our lives and schedules, we will become strong women of God who can resist temptation, persevere in trial, and pass our tests of faith with flying colors. We will then be able to join the Proverbs 31 woman and smile at our future—free from fear, worry, and anxiety.

I, myself, look to God regularly in times of need. Tonight, for example, frustration had mounted in my spirit all week long as normal life consumed me, and I had not completed everything on my to-do list. Between sending Jim and Rachel off to the Ukraine on an 11-day ministry trip, driving James to multiple lessons and drivers' education classes, taking my mom to several doctors' appointments, and assisting mom and dad with numerous tasks as they completed their move into our apartment, I had not gotten my own work done. But, in the mist of my agitation, I decided to forego the to-do list and join Molly and her friend as they worshiped in the living room.

As I sat in God's presence, His peace washed over me and I was able to give Him all of my frustrations. It was there that I gained a new understanding of what Jesus meant when He commended Mary for taking time to sit at His feet. I had always resented the story of Mary and Martha, feeling like it condemned Martha-type people like me who tend to be workers. But, tonight, I realized that Jesus was commending Mary because she was willing to lay down her work, sit at His feet, listen, and rest. We all need this. As moms, there will always be more work for us to do. But, unless we learn to sit at His feet, we will get worn out and end up complaining because no one is helping us—which is exactly what Martha did.

John Mulinde and Mark Daniel of World Trumpet Mission have taught us much about saturating in the Word and building altars to God in our homes. (Altars are times when we gather as a family and court God's presence with worship.) If we compare our daily lives to a sack, these teachers exhort us to empty every activity from the sack. Then, the first thing we should put back into our sack is time with the Lord. When this is accomplished, then we can fill our days with whatever else fits in. So often we do the opposite, and our days become so full of other things that there is no room for Him.

Time with God is the most important thing we can do each day. His Word will teach, instruct, train, and correct us. As we pour out our worries and concerns, His peace will cover us. Our praise will exalt Him as Lord over our problems. The result? We will become strong women of God who will be a blessing to our husbands, families, and those around us.

Questions for personal use or group discussion:

1. As a mother, describe your frustrations and successes in taking time with the Lord.
2. Without strength from the Lord, we may struggle in the following areas: laziness, inability to resist temptation or attacks, discouragement, lack of vision, deadness of spirit, etc. Are any of these areas of weakness for you? Explain.
3. If not the Lord, what source do you typically turn to when you feel soul-hunger or thirst? Explain.
4. To what extent do you tend to depend on others for your spiritual strength? Explain.
5. In what ways did the story of Marjorie Newlin speak to you? Explain.

Chapter 10

Fear Not

...casting all your anxiety on Him, because He cares for you (1 Peter 5:7).

As we have already learned, women have a different calling than men—not a lesser calling, but a different one. We also process life's events differently. Let's glean some examples of this from stories about Mary, Jesus' mother.

In Luke 2, we read the story of Mary giving birth to Jesus in the stable. The angels announced His birth to the shepherds in the field. The shepherds, after proceeding to Bethlehem, told Mary all that the angels had told them concerning her son. "*But Mary treasured up all these things, pondering them in her heart*" (Luke 2:19).

In another circumstance, Mary responded in a similar manner. Jesus' family was in Jerusalem attending the Passover Feast. As everyone returned home, Mary and Joseph realized that 12-year-old Jesus was not with their group. After frantically looking for Him for three days, they finally found Jesus in the temple talking with the teachers. Mary exclaimed, *"Son, why have You treated us this way? Behold, your father and I have been anxiously looking for You."* Jesus answered, *"Did you not know that I had to be in my Father's house?"...and His mother treasured all these things in her heart"* (Luke 2:48-49, 51).

Twice we are told Mary heard all that was said about Jesus and she treasured these things, pondering them in her heart. Scripture could have easily told us that *both* Joseph and Mary treasured these things in their hearts. But, no, only Mary's name is mentioned in both cases. I believe women do a lot more "treasuring" and "pondering" about life's events than do men.

I'd like to share an example from my own life that demonstrates this difference between men and women. Many years ago, while attending a church conference, a young man from another state approached Jim and asked to meet with him. They met for coffee that same afternoon. Later on, as we got ready for bed, I asked, "Why did Bryan want to meet with you today?"

Jim answered casually, "Oh, he told me he was interested in Bethany and thinks she might be the one he is supposed to marry." Then he promptly fell asleep. But, this was monumental news for me since none of our children had dated and none were yet married. I couldn't believe someone was interested in one of my daughters! As Jim slept soundly beside me, I was awake most of the night pondering this new development. I pictured future weddings and thought of romance, relationships, and lots of other related topics. As it turned out, that particular relationship never came to pass, and Bethany is now happily married to David. But, my story illustrates the intricate way our female minds work and how Jim and I, as a man and woman, responded very differently to that situation.

One positive result of the pondering and treasuring is that, if handled correctly, both lead us to prayer and intercession for situations and for those we love. Conversely, when not handled the right way, our thoughts can lead to fear and worry. In fact, fear and worry strive to become our constant companions. Webster tells us that *fear* is "the expectation of evil or impending danger—the thought of future evil likely to befall us." *Worry* is "a state of anxiety and uncertainty over actual or potential problems."

I worry about many things. Over the years, I've worried plenty about finances and provision. My other greatest concern has been my children—their physical, emotional, social, and spiritual needs—in all different stages of their lives. When my children were young, I worried about my ability to properly care for them and train them. As they've gotten older, I've worried about their futures—who they will marry and what path they will take.

Jim observes that once a woman gets pregnant and goes into labor to deliver her child, she "carries" her children for the rest of her life in her heart and never quits "laboring" over them to see them grow, mature, and succeed. I am not saying men do not have worries and concerns. Nor am I saying men do not care about their children's lives. However, I believe women do both on a whole different level than men. I have asked Jim, "Do you think about our children a lot?" He has responded, "Yes, I think about our children, but not to the extent that you do, as their mother."

It is apparent the Proverbs 31 woman was not ruled by fear and worry as...*she smiles at the future* (Proverbs 31:25).

She was obviously not expecting future evil to befall her or her family. She did, however, exhibit a healthy kind of fear: *A woman who fears the Lord, she shall be praised* (Proverbs 31:30).

> **By strengthening ourselves in the**
> **Lord, we will walk in the fear of God.**
> **Our lives will subsequently be marked**
> **by trust, not fear and anxiety.**

As with many other areas of my life, the Word of God has been the key to my success over fear. *Don't fret or worry. Instead of worrying, pray. Let petitions and praises shape your worries into prayers, letting God know your concerns. Before you know it, a sense of God's wholeness, everything coming together for good, will come and settle you down. It's wonderful what happens when Christ displaces worry at the center of your life* (Philippians 4:6-7, TMB). *Humble yourselves, therefore, under the mighty hand of God, that He may exalt you at the proper time, casting all your anxiety upon Him, because He cares for you* (1 Peter 5:6-7). These are good places to start: turn your worries into prayers and cast all your anxiety on God. Time and time again these verses have encouraged me to turn my concerns and worries over to Him. When I do that, His peace settles in my heart.

One day, God opened up a passage of Scripture that brought great victory to me in the area of fear about my children. *You have searched me and known me! You know when I sit down and when I rise up; You discern my thoughts from afar. You search out my path and my lying down, and are acquainted with all my ways. Even before a word is on my tongue, behold, O Lord, you know it altogether. You hem me in behind and before, and lay your hand upon me....In Your book were written, every one of them, the days that were formed for me, when as yet there was none of the* (Psalm 139:1-6, ESV).

As I turn these verses into prayerful affirmations over my children's lives, fear melts away. Following is a prayer I have prayed over my older children using these verses as my guide: *Lord, You are intimately involved in my children's lives. You are acquainted with everything about them. You know their needs and struggles. You understand their thoughts and fears. You know everything about their futures—what lies before them, the decisions they must make, and what is best for them. You go before them into their futures—they don't go alone. You know their need for life direction and for godly, Kingdom spouses. You will lead, guide, and direct them. I don't have to be afraid for their futures. You have laid your hand upon them—Your powerful, wise, mighty, capable, loving, sufficient, gracious, and merciful hand. You have a plan and purpose for their lives. They do not have to figure it out on their own. You have answers for them. Thank you, Lord, that You are sufficient for every need my children have.*

This may sound silly, but I get afraid and panicky when my children are lonely or bored. I often feel helpless to meet those needs. So I pray. God's Word tells us that He knows our needs even before we ask. He instructs us to pray this way: "*Give us this day our daily bread*" (Matthew 6:11). I believe our daily bread consists of more than food since God created us with physical, emotional, social, and spiritual needs. Therefore, I ask Him to satisfy the daily needs of my children in all those areas. And, when they are bored, we command boredom to get out of our house and ask God's spirit of creativity to be activated within them. It's amazing to see how God has faithfully answered those prayers over the years.

I've also been fearful in the area of finances and provision—themes that are near the top of everyone's "fear list." What does the Word of God have to say about this need?

How have I used His Word to strengthen myself? And, how can you do the same?

In 1990, Jim left his full-time job with the local utility company—a job that provided a nice retirement plan and medical benefits—to launch Lifeline Ministries, a non-profit ministry. We went from receiving a regular paycheck to, as Jim calls it, "living out of the mailbox." We were then (and have been ever since) completely dependent on speaking honorariums and the support of individuals and churches. What we did may have appeared to be a foolish decision to some since we had five small children at home. However, we clearly knew this was a decision God was leading us to make. Nonetheless, I've had many, many seasons over the past years when I've been fearful about a lack of finance. Thankfully, though, that fear thrust me into the Word of God where I learned to cling to His promises. Day after day I turned to all of my favorite verses on provision, praying them over our lives and writing them out in my journal. In fact, I have entire journals filled mostly with "provision verses."

One of my favorites about provision says this: *"Do not be anxious then, saying, 'What shall we eat?' or 'What shall we drink?' or 'With what shall we clothe ourselves?' For all these things the Gentiles eagerly seek; for your heavenly Father knows that you need all these things. But seek first His kingdom and His righteousness; and all these things shall be added to you. Therefore do not be anxious for tomorrow, for tomorrow will care for itself"* (Mathew 6:31-34). This promise of provision is conditional. God promises to meet our needs *if* we are seeking Him and His kingdom first. If we can honestly say this is so, then we can be assured He will take care of us. It is comforting to know that He sees and is fully aware of our needs—even before we ask. He gives us permission to come to Him with our needs, promises to meet them, and tells us not to worry. God did not lead the Israelites out of Egypt and promise to bring them to the Promised Land only to let them die of hunger and thirst in the desert. The same is true for us.

Fear of the future has also been a regular visitor in my life. This verse has ministered to me greatly: *Trust in the Lord with all your heart, and do not lean on your own understanding. In all your ways acknowledge Him, and He will make your paths straight* (Proverbs 3:5-6). How have I prayed using this verse? *Lord, I acknowledge Your greatness, power, and wisdom. I declare that You are sufficient for every situation and need in my life. Thank you that you promise to make all of our paths straight and clear. Thank you that You are with us every step of the way—just as You were with the Israelites in the desert.*

This verse has also been helpful in my battle against fear: *But I trust in You, O Lord; I say, "You are my God." My times are in Your hand* (Psalm 31:14-15 ESV). How comforting it is to know that my life, the life of my family, and the lives of our children are in God's hands. This verse brings to mind a scene out of an old Disney movie, *Honey, I Shrunk the Kids*, where a would-be-scientist dad mistakenly shrinks his children. One scene shows the normal-sized dad holding his miniature children in his hands. That is the reality of our lives in God's hands—our miniature, impotent lives resting in His huge, all-sufficient hands. What a confidence-inspiring picture!

Fear can also surface from some unexpected sources. Most husbands will, at some point in their lives, make a poor decision that results in negative consequences for their wives and families. These decisions can put us in a precarious position that can easily lead to fear. Even Sarah, the wife of godly Abraham, was the unfortunate recipient of some very poor decisions Abraham made. Let's examine how her life can speak to us today.

In the same way, you wives, be submissive to your own husbands so that even if any of them are disobedient to the Word, they may be won without a word by the behavior of their wives, as they observe your chaste and respectful behavior…For in this way in former times the holy women also, who hoped in God, used to adorn themselves, being submissive to their own husbands. Thus Sarah obeyed Abraham, calling him lord, and you have become her children if you do what is right without being frightened by any fear (1 Peter 3:1-2, 5-6). Abraham was the man God chose to bring blessing to the whole earth. What decisions did this godly man make that caused Sarah to be frightened? How did she respond? Thank goodness the Bible is full of honest stories about real people—sinners like ourselves—that can help us in the circumstances we face.

In Genesis 12:1, we read the first words of God to Abraham: *"Go forth from your country, and from your relatives, and from your father's house, to the land which I will show you."* Abraham's obedience to that call was enough to create fear in Sarah. In submitting herself to her husband's call, she was supposed to leave everything—her family, house, and country—and face the great unknown. Not only did she have to deal with fear, she undoubtedly experienced great sorrow at the loss of everything dear to her.

But, an even greater cause for fear—and an opportunity to trust in God—came to Sarah as she and Abraham traveled to their new home. Not once, but twice, Abraham's deception greatly jeopardized Sarah's safety and well-being. Both Genesis 12:11-20 and Genesis 20:1-18 tell similar stories: Since Sarah was a very beautiful woman, Abraham was fearful that the kings of the foreign nations they traveled through would kill him in order to take Sarah for themselves. Attempting to spare his own life, he asked Sarah to say that she was his sister, not his wife.

(She was his half-sister, as she was the daughter of his father. However, to ask her to admit to only half the truth was cowardly on Abraham's part.) Upon hearing Abraham and Sarah's half-truth, two different kings took Sarah into their possession. I can't imagine the fear that must have assaulted her in both instances. She could have easily been raped or violated—all because of her husband's deception and cowardice. Thankfully, in both cases, God intervened on Sarah's behalf, and she was spared violation and restored unharmed to her husband. These stories shed a whole new light on the verses we just read from 1 Peter 3 about Sarah submitting to her husband, hoping in God, and not giving way to fear.

Two keys are found in these verses: Sarah hoped in God (1 Peter 3:5), and she was not frightened by any fear (1 Peter 3:6). In the midst of Abraham's failure, Sarah hoped in God. In other words, she strengthened herself in God since her husband had not protected her. The result was that she was not frightened at all—even though she was held captive by a foreign ruler and could easily have been violated at any moment. Amazing! Incredulously, Abraham allowed this scenario to play out twice! Two times Sarah's husband failed her, and she had to strengthen herself in God. Wonderfully, God heard her cries and rescued her both times.

We are married to imperfect husbands who are sinners, just as we are. It is inevitable that they will make decisions that sometimes put us in jeopardy—hopefully, though, not to the extent that Sarah's safety was jeopardized! (I am, by no means, suggesting that any woman should remain in a situation potentially harmful to her or her children.) Our husbands may make poor financial decisions. They may make career moves that don't portend well for the family. There are many decisions they make that could potentially put us in a fearful position. If this happens, we have a choice to make. We can either give way to hysteria and fear. Or, we can be like Sarah who hoped in God and overcame fear.

With Jim's permission, I'll talk about a situation in our own lives related to this topic. Contrary to my counsel, Jim made a financial investment that eventually failed and put us in debt. It was one of those "too-good-to-be-true" investments. I've struggled with his decision and the ensuing debt we've accrued due to his mistake. I did not react to Jim's poor judgment as graciously as Sarah apparently did with Abraham's deceit. I've had feelings of anger toward Jim, and I've also succumbed to fear at times because of the debt and financial pressure that resulted.

In the midst of my anger and fear, I have had to go to God. Where my husband failed us, I have asked God to intervene. I admit that Jim did not make this decision maliciously. He proceeded with the investment because he was looking for a way to bless our family financially. In light of that, I have appealed to God's mercy and asked Him to help us get out of this debt, even though it is our own fault. I admit that I've not dealt with this situation in an exemplary manner. However, I'm learning to trust God, just as Sarah did.

We will all have ample opportunity in life to give in to fear. But, remember that fear makes us weak. As women of God, it does not look good on us. We will be characterized by trust and strength as we learn to regularly pour out our fears, worries, and concerns to God and then saturate our lives with His Word and promises. The truth of His Word will make us strong. His truth will give us victory over fear and anxiety, and this will look very good on us, indeed.

Questions for personal use or group discussion:

1. Can you relate to Mary's "treasuring and pondering" of life's events? Explain.
2. Does the pondering and treasuring tend to lead you to prayer and intercession or to fear and worry? Think of an example.
3. What is at the top of your "fear list"? What verses from the Bible help you most in overcoming those fears?
4. What are your greatest fears about your children?
5. How have you handled poor decisions made by your husband? (Please share with discretion, if in a group!) How would the Lord have you respond in that situation?

Chapter 11

Children

In denying our children, we deny the best of ourselves.
Many potential parents chose childlessness for the sake
of their freedom, but hedging our bets and hoarding
our pleasures are not marks of freedom. Instead, they
are the essence of fear.[56] –Janie Cheaney

A book on motherhood would be incomplete without a chapter on children. I explored the topic of children in depth in my first book *Are All Those Children Yours?* I will highlight truths from that book in this chapter because those truths bear repeating. They have altered the course of my life and shaped my priorities and values like no other. Allow me to share our journey of revelation.

We are the parents of eight. The sheer numbers in our family evoked a lot of different responses over the years. We experienced loving, approving looks from older people who grew up in a generation where big families were the norm. At times, we got what my husband calls the "environmental glare" from the "save-the-earth types," as if we didn't care about our planet. Grocery clerks asked if I was buying for commercial use when I did my weekly shopping. We received lots of stares and head counting from occupants of other cars as we traveled down the highway in our 15-passenger van on vacations. Once, we even had someone in a pickup swing a used condom out their window as they passed by, as if to offer a solution to our "problem."

Jim and I did not plan on having eight children. In fact, as I shared earlier, I was an unlikely candidate to be the mother of a large family. I don't remember ever talking about how many children we wanted to have. But, after two years of adjusting to marriage, we felt ready to start a family. Allison, our first-born, arrived shortly before our third anniversary. Motherhood was a huge adjustment for me as *everything* in my life changed. I went to the grocery store when Allison was about a week old and felt like everyone was staring at me. I was certain they knew something momentous had just happened in my life, and I wanted to shout, "I'm not the same person you used to see in here. I'm different now. You don't know what I've just been through!" It took almost one-and-a-half years before life resumed some semblance of normalcy for me, even though Allison was a very easy baby.

When Allison was 27-months old, I gave birth to Bethany. Motherhood was more natural for me by then, and I had more confidence. But, as is the case with most mothers of small children, I struggled with fatigue and often felt overwhelmed and discouraged. Jim did what he could to help, but knowing I would struggle without clear vision for my calling, he encouraged me to read Christian books on motherhood, especially during the low points.

At one such point, I headed to the Christian bookstore and came home with a book by Mary Pride entitled *The Way Home: Beyond Feminism, Back to Reality.* God used that book to change our lives. Pride explained how the world's view of children had infiltrated the church and how we, as Christians, believed more what the world said about children than what God said. Both Jim and I were challenged to evaluate what we believed and how we were living. We had not really thought through the issue of contraception before, nor had we considered Pride's contention that children are a blessing. We were both able to embrace this new truth and, in faith, made a decision to leave the rest of our family-planning to God. We were willing to trust Him and receive the full blessing He wanted to pour out to us.

Following are some portions of Scripture that have been life-changing for us: *Behold, children are a gift of the Lord; the fruit of the womb is a reward. Like arrows in the hand of a warrior, so are the children of one's youth. How blessed is the man whose quiver is full of them; they shall not be ashamed when they speak with their enemies in the gate* (Psalm 127:3-5). Since God is God, He could have chosen any words He wanted to describe children. So, it is highly significant He chose these words: gift, fruit, reward, and blessing. God also likens children to the arrows of a warrior, signifying their invaluable resource in spiritual warfare.

The connection between children and blessing is further confirmed by observing the blessings and curses God pronounces on His people based on their obedience or disobedience. Hosea describes God's curse this way: *Their glory will fly away like a bird—no birth, no pregnancy, and no conception! Though they bring up their children, yet I will bereave them until not a man is left…Give them a miscarrying womb and dry breasts…Even though they bear children, I will slay the precious ones of their womb* (Hosea 9: 11-14, 16). Among other things, judgment involves no birth, no pregnancy, no conception, miscarrying wombs, dry breasts, and the death of their children. Other verses in the context of judgment declare the same thing: *"I will bereave them of children"* (Jeremiah 15:7). And, *Give their children over to famine, and deliver them up to the power of the sword, and let their wives become childless and widowed* (Jeremiah 18:21). Each time, God's judgment is manifested by barrenness and loss of children.

God's blessing, on the other hand, always shows itself through open wombs and an abundance of children. Psalms expresses the blessing of God upon the man who fears Him in this way: *Your wife shall be like a fruitful vine within your house, your children like olive plants around your table* (Psalm128:3). A vine is considered fruitful if it bears lots of fruit. And, olive plants were considered a sign of wealth in Bible times. No farmer wants a fruitless vine or a single olive plant. Again, children are linked to blessing and fruitfulness.

In Deuteronomy, we see similar blessings on those who fully follow God: *"And He will love you and bless you and multiply you. He will also bless the fruit of your womb and the fruit of your ground… You shall be blessed above all peoples; there shall be no male or female barren among you or among your cattle"* (Deuteronomy 7:12-16). The theme of blessing equates with an abundance of children, and this abounds in Scripture.

Not only are children an individual blessing, but they are also a blessing to a nation: *In a multitude of people is a king's glory, but in the dearth of people is a prince's ruin* (Proverbs 14:28). A large population is an asset to society. It guarantees a large work force, a healthy economy, and an adequate army for defense.

Contrary to biblical wisdom, though, many parents severely limit the number of children they have around the world. The birth rate in Europe is 1.38, much lower than 2.1 which is the rate needed for societal survival. With dwindling populations, the economies of certain nations are currently on the brink of bankruptcy. To reverse this crisis, some governments are now paying parents to have more children.[57] Take, for example, the Russian holiday that was instituted to combat the demographic crisis former President Vladimir Putin called the most urgent problem facing Russia. September 12th is designated as the Day of Conception. To encourage participation, couples are given time off of work to procreate. Those who give birth on June 12th are awarded prizes by regional governments. Those prizes have ranged from a sports utility vehicle to, video cameras, televisions, refrigerators, or washing machines.[58] This is an example of man's ways going awry when God's truth is rejected.

When nations reject God, they also reject His truth. Rejection of His blessing of children is pervasive. Consider one of the primary solutions offered by industrialized nations to solve poverty in third-world countries: contraception and abortion. Instead of viewed as a blessing, children are often deemed the source of a lot of the world's problems. This specific attempt to solve poverty is very misguided. Deuteronomy 28 tells us that poverty is the result of idol-worship. Proverbs reveals another cause of poverty: *Abundant food is in the fallow ground of the poor, but it is swept away by injustice* (Proverbs 13:23). Too many children are not the cause of poverty in nations. Poverty is caused by idol-worship and injustice. Only as we are grounded in God's Word will we have accurate answers for the world's problems.

As we have already seen, Scripture is very clear that both an abundance of children and an open, fruitful womb are blessings. It is equally clear that God is the Lord of conception and birth. I give full credit to Rick and Jan Hess's book *A Full Quiver* for opening my eyes to the following conception stories in the Bible.

First, consider the story of Abraham and Sarah in Genesis 20—a story we already explored in the chapter "Fear Not." Abraham lied to Abimelech, king of Gerar and told him his beautiful wife Sarah was only his sister. When Abimelech took Sarah into his own home, the Lord closed every womb in Abimelech's household as judgment for taking another man's wife. When the truth about Sarah came out, *Abraham prayed to God; and God healed Abimelech and his wife and his maids, so that they bore children. For the Lord had closed fast all the wombs of the household of Abimelech because of Sarah, Abraham's wife* (Genesis 20:17). In this story, God closed wombs, and He opened wombs.[59]

The story of Rachel and Leah in Genesis 29-30 illustrates the same point. Jacob loved his wife Rachel but had been tricked into marrying Leah, her older sister. *Now the Lord saw that Leah was unloved, and He opened her womb, but Rachel was barren* (Genesis 29:31). Leah bore a son and went on to bear four sons in a row. Then she stopped.

Rachel, angered by her own barrenness and jealous of her sister's fertility, demanded that her husband give her children. Jacob responded this way: *"Am I in the place of God, who has withheld from you the fruit of the womb"* (Genesis 30:2)? As the story progressed, both sisters used their maids to obtain more children. Later, *God gave heed to Leah, and she conceived and bore Jacob a fifth son* (Genesis 30:17-21). He was followed by another son and then Leah's first daughter—seven children in all. Finally, *God remembered Rachel, and God gave heed to her and opened her womb* (Genesis 30:22). Clearly, throughout this entire sequence, God not only opened and closed wombs, He also determined the timing and spacing of children.[60]

Further evidence of God's sovereignty over conception is found in the story of Hannah. The Lord had closed her womb. As Hannah cried out to God, He heard her prayers and...*the Lord remembered her and it came about in due time, after Hannah had conceived, that she gave birth to a son* (1 Samuel 1:19-20).[61] In every case I have cited, God opened and closed wombs. He is the Lord of all things, including conception and birth. What a novel thought that *God* is in control of our fertility! Most people in today's enlightened society assume *they* are in control of their fertility.

Many people fear that if they leave family planning to chance or to God they will breed like rabbits! My own parents are a good example that that is not always true. Mom and Dad both came from families with six children each and wanted a large family themselves. Although they never used birth control, it was five years into their marriage before I was conceived. Thirteen months later, my mom gave birth to my sister. They never had any more children. Few women would willingly choose to get pregnant again four months after giving birth. However, if my mother had not left herself open to that possibility, I would have been an only child. God has a special plan and purpose for each couple. He can be trusted to know what is best for each of us.

I do not share all of this to put a burden of guilt or frustration on those who struggle with infertility. Jesus came to reverse every curse—including the curse of barrenness. We need to stand with and encourage those who are barren. On one of our ministry trips to Russia, we were praying for a barren couple. In the midst of praying, the Lord gave me this thought: *"Not yet" does not mean "never."* He, the God of the impossible, is also the God of conception and birth. We can trust His timing and His perfect will for our lives.

We need large doses of God's truth about children to combat the pervasive lies with which we are constantly bombarded. Whereas God's Word tells us that a man with a lot of children is wealthy, the world says that children are expensive and that we can't possibly afford more than one or two. Take, for example, the following quote by actress Angelina Jolie, partner of actor Brad Pitt: "Brad and I want to continue to adopt, but keeping a big family uses up a lot of money." At that time, the multimillionaire couple had three children.[62] If Brad and Angelina can't afford more children, some parents may reason, *How can we?* Annual statistics—reporting that it costs $160,000-$367,000 to raise a child from birth through age 17[63]—also cause fear in prospective parents. Few people stop to think that these figures are highly inflated.

Or, note the strong bias against children in this article: "In the interest of preserving our planet and species, shouldn't religious organizations be encouraging smaller families? How should people of faith respond to the gathering environmental storm? First, we must stop having so many children. Clergy should consider voicing the difficult truth that having more than two children during such a time is selfish. Dare we say, even sinful?"[64] Here, the voice of the world says that only two children or less should be tolerated. To combat that, we need the truth of God's Word: *Like arrows in the hands of a warrior, so are the children of one's youth. How blessed is the man whose quiver is full of them* (Psalm 127:3-4).

This anti-child spirit was not strong in past generations. As a result, many couples produced world-changers in their fruitfulness. Charles Finney, the great evangelist of the 1800s, was the seventh of seven children in his family. John & Charles Wesley were the 14th and 17th children of Susanna Wesley. They were great revivalists of the 1700s, mightily used by God in England and the United States. George Whitefield, also a seventh child, was instrumental in the First Great Awakening in the 1700s. Jonathan Edwards, who preached the famous sermon "Sinners in the Hands of an Angry God," was the 11th of 11 children.[65] Think how the purposes of God would have been thwarted in the earth had their parents closed their wombs prematurely!

I will close with an excerpt from *Mother*, a classic book by Kathleen Norris, originally printed in 1911. It is the story of Margaret, a young woman who grew discontent within the confines of her home and began to despise the role of motherhood and homemaking. Her own mother had given birth to eight children. Bruce was born first. Charles, the second-born, had died. Margaret was third. She hated the hard work and strain on finances that a large family created. Then begins the journey of her heart on its way back home. Following is a portion of the story describing a revelation Margaret received as her heart began to turn:

> She had sometimes wished, or half-formed the wish, that she and Bruce had been the only ones! Yes, came the sudden thought, but it wouldn't have been Bruce and Margaret after all. It would have been Bruce and Charles. With a sickening thud of her heart, Margaret understood that that was what women did, then,

when they denied the right-of-life to the distant, unwanted, possible little person! Calmly, constantly, in all placid philosophy and self-justification, they kept from the world not only the troublesome new baby—with his tears and his illnesses, his endless claim on mind and body and spirit—but perhaps the flowing beauty of Rebecca, or the buoyant indomitable spirit of a small Robert, whose grip on life, whose energy and ambition were as strong as Margaret's own. It seemed perfectly incredible, it seemed perfectly impossible that if Mother had had only the two—and how many thousands of women didn't have that!—she, Margaret, a pronounced and separate entity, traveled, ambitious, and to become the wife of one of the world's great men, might not have been lying here in the summer night![66]

On her journey, Margaret discovered a potential suitor, Dr. John Tenison. Humiliated by her common family and humble home, she shied away from introducing him to her parents. Unbeknownst to her, Dr. Tenison had already met her parents and greatly admired them both. Listen to him gently correct the wrong perception Margaret had of her mother (and her family):

"You know," he went on musingly, "these days when women just serenely ignore the question of children, or at most, as a special concession, bring up one or two— just the one or two whose expenses can be comfortably met!—there's something magnificent in a woman like your mother, who begins eight destinies instead of one! She doesn't strain and chafe to express herself through the medium of poetry or music or the stage, but she puts her whole splendid philosophy into her nursery—and launches sound little bodies and minds that have their first growth cleanly and purely about her knees. Responsibility— that's what these other women are afraid of! But it seems to me there is no responsibility like that of decreeing that young lives simply shall not be. Why, what good is learning, or elegance of manner, or painfully acquired fitness of speech and taste and point of view, if you are not going to distil it into the growing plants, the only real hope we have in the world? You know, Miss Paget, there is a higher tribunal than the social tribunal of

this world after all; and it seems to
me that a woman who stands there,
as your mother will, with a forest of
new lives about her, and a record
like hers, will—will find she has a
Friend at court!" he said, smiling.[67]

That, in a very condensed form, is why we have eight children. When confronted with God's truth about children, we chose to gladly put our fertility and family size in His loving and wise hands. (God closed my womb after James, our eighth, was born.) As a result, my last 30-plus years have been filled with many sleep-deprived nights; loads of laundry; huge grocery bills; and countless trips to ballet classes, youth group, and music lessons. However, our lives have been, and continue to be, filled with great joy and a sense that we have discovered one of God's greatest riches.

Margaret came to the realization that life would have been robbed of much if any one of her siblings had not been born. The same is true for Jim and me. Each of our eight children, with their unique personality and gifting, is bursting with potential and dreams. Our lives would be impoverished if any one of them had not been born. So, also, the world would be impoverished without them and the contributions each of them will make. (The same is true of your children.) There is no telling what impact our children and subsequent generations will have on history, the world, and eternity. We are so thankful that God's truth showed us the path of life.

Questions for personal use or group discussion:

1. What are your first thoughts when you hear of or see a large family? What is the source of your perspective?

2. How many children were in your family growing up? Did your family experience affect your decision about how many children you wanted to have? Explain.

3. Is your view of children more impacted by the world's perspective or God's truth? Explain.

4. How did the conception stories from the Bible impact your thinking? Explain.

5. List some worldly lies (and their sources) that have affected your view of children and the family-planning decisions you have made.

6. Evaluate and discuss the following quote: *In denying our children, we deny the best of ourselves. Many potential parents chose childlessness for the sake of their freedom, but hedging our bets and hoarding our pleasures are not marks of freedom. Instead, they are the essence of fear.*

Chapter 12

Revival and Reformation

Christian mothers carry their children in hostile
territory. When you are in public with them, you are
standing with, and defending, the objects of cultural
dislike. You are publicly testifying that you value
what God values, and that you refuse to value what
the world values...You represent everything that our
culture hates, because you represent laying down your
life for another—and laying down your life for another
represents the Gospel.[68] –Rachel Jankovic

When mothers and homemakers faithfully fulfill their calling, they directly strengthen the basic building block of society—the family. Conversely, when this place of dominion is neglected or abandoned, the strength and health of the family is severely undermined. We, as keepers of the home, are a key to the wellness of the nation through our role of building strong families. The following quote from author Andy Crouch reinforces this point:

> **"I wanted mothers to realize the basic unit of culture is the family, and what happens in those first five years shapes people for the rest of their lives. That's as much culture-making as anything that happens in the White House or on Fifth Avenue."[69]**

Going deeper, just as the family is the basic building block of society, the building block of the family is its individual members. Mothers and homemakers have direct influence on these individual members. As we support and encourage our husbands and raise healthy, whole children, we have enormous influence—influence that impacts the world, history, and the Kingdom of God.

Today, it appears that our nation has stubbornly and defiantly turned its back on God and His ways. Scripture is very clear that when we abandon God, He abandons us. Many believe that our culture is currently living under God's curse instead of His blessing, as shown by our disintegrating families and society. The fact is, we are in dire need of revival—"recovery to life from death"—and reformation—"changing from bad to good."[70]

God's Word reveals formulas for revival and reformation that instruct us how to move from death to life and from bad to good. One of those well-known how-to's is found in 2 Chronicles 7:14: "*If my people who are called by My name humble themselves and pray, and seek My face and turn from their wicked ways, then I will hear from heaven, will forgive their sin, and will heal their land.*"

This is pretty clear: humble ourselves, pray, turn around, and seek His face. In return, He promises to heal our land and this will result in revival and reformation—a move from death to life and curse to blessing.

Another of God's formulas for revival and reformation is tucked away in a verse many of us know quite well but may overlook as a key to our nation's healing. *"Behold I am going to send you Elijah the prophet before the coming of the great and terrible day of the Lord. And he will restore the hearts of the fathers to their children, and the hearts of the children to their fathers, lest I come and smite the land with a curse"* (Malachi 4:5-6). Let's look at this verse more closely and discover what it means for motherhood and homemaking.

Positively said, this verse would read: "When the hearts of fathers are turned toward their children and the hearts of children are turned toward their fathers, our land experiences blessing—a revived and reformed culture." Or, conversely, it would sound like this: "When fathers turn their hearts away from their children and children turn their hearts away from their fathers, we live under a curse—a nation under judgment."

Why does this verse solely address the hearts of fathers? There could be two possible explanations. First, the hearts of mothers are possibly not addressed because this is already their primary calling and therefore only fathers need to be addressed. Or, it is also possible that just as *man* in Scripture can mean "men and women," *father* here could mean both "father and mother." Either way, it's obvious that one way a nation can obtain God's blessing is for both mothers and fathers to turn their hearts toward their children.

Webster defines *heart* as "the chief part." God knows our children need us to turn the chief part of who we are to them in order that they become whole people. Then, as whole people, they can become change agents who scale the mountains of influence in our culture and work to see God's will accomplished on the earth.

Giving children our hearts, the chief part of who we are, is in complete agreement with other words from Scripture: *"And these words which I am commanding you today, shall be on your heart and you shall teach them diligently to your sons and shall talk of them when you sit in your house and when you walk by the way and when you lie down and when you rise up"* (Deuteronomy 6:6-7). Again, God makes it obvious to us that our priority in life is our children, teaching them by our words, life, and example. Unfortunately, the modern American family spends such little time together that most of this teaching and training comes from others.

We have seen that our faithful dominion in the home has a two-fold effect. First, we impact the health and strength of the basic building block of society. Second, our influence is multiplied as we raise whole children who become change-agents on the mountains of influence in culture.

Let's look further at this process of raising world-changers. It's helpful to understand Maslow's Hierarchy of Needs Theory. Maslow defined the basic needs of people: physiological needs, needs for safety and security, needs for love and belonging, needs for esteem, and the need for self-actualization. He views the first four needs as essential survival needs.

- The physiological needs include the necessity for air, water, sleep, the right temperature, food, etc. Obviously, these are the basic survival needs. But, we need much more than these things to live. This is illustrated by babies in orphanages whose basic needs are met but who die simply because they are never held or loved.

- Safety and security needs come next. Once the physiological requisites are met, we become increasingly interested in finding safe circumstances, stability, and protection. When these are not met, we feel fear and anxiety.

- Our next greatest need is for love and belonging— friends, a sweetheart, children, affectionate relationships in general, and even a sense of community. When this is unmet, we become susceptible to loneliness and social anxieties.

- Then we begin to look for self-esteem. Maslow noted two versions of esteem needs. The lower version is the need for the respect of others—the need for status, fame, glory, recognition, attention, reputation, appreciation, dignity, and even dominance. The higher form involves the need for self-respect—confidence, competence, achievement, mastery, independence, and freedom. Low self-esteem and inferiority complexes result when these needs are not met.

- Once the previous four conditions have been met, self-actualization is then possible. Self-actualization includes morality, creativity, spontaneity, problem solving, and a lack of prejudice.

We move through these levels a bit like stages to attain a healthy overall development. If a person has significant problems in the course of development (i.e. a period of extreme insecurity or hunger as a child, the loss of a family member through death or divorce, or significant neglect or abuse) that individual may fixate on that set of needs for the rest of his life and find it difficult to move forward. These individuals may be ruled by fear, social anxieties, low self-esteem, or inferiority complexes.[71] In short, these are not the qualities of a world-changer!

When the lower needs are successfully met, a person is capable of reaching the last level—their highest potential. The world calls this "self actualization." Christians view it as fulfilling our destiny in God. In other words, these people have the potential to be change-agents on the mountains of culture.

So, how do we raise world-changers? One of the primary ways of doing this is through giving the chief part of who we are to our children. When we do that, our children's basic needs will be successfully met and they will be favorably positioned to walk in their God-given potential.

First, we meet our children's basic physiological needs. Then, they learn trust. A wonderful verse in the Bible speaks to this: *Thou didst make me trust when upon my mother's breasts* (Psalm 22:9). Nursing is one of the primary God-given avenues by which children learn that the world is a safe place where their needs will consistently be met. In our culture, mothers often only nurse their babies for six months or less. In biblical culture, however, women commonly nursed their babies until they were two or three years of age. Moms were in close proximity to their babies all that time, building trust, safety, and security into their spirits.

I've been reminded of a child's needs as I've watched my two oldest daughters mother their children. I periodically babysit Allison's children so she can run errands. She can rarely leave, though, for more than two hours at a time when her children are infants. She has to time her errands around the baby's nursing schedule. Nursing guarantees that mom has to stay close by her baby. Many view this as a burdensome hindrance. But, I believe nursing is God's wise design, ensuring that mothers meet the needs of safety and security in their babies.

Allow me to say a word about formula-feeding versus breastfeeding. In His wisdom, God designed women with breasts to nurse their babies. He designed breast milk to perfectly meet the nutritional needs of babies and give them natural immunity to disease. Man, in his "wisdom," invented formula. I'm not saying we should never use formula. In fact, I had to switch to formula-feeding for two of my babies because I was not producing enough milk. Formula is a blessing in many respects. However, one downside to the use of formula is that it has enabled mothers to be gone from their infants for long periods of time, either for work or other reasons. This deprives babies of the greatest source of love and affirmation they have—their mothers. No one else (not even a grandmother) loves a baby like his mother. In this instance, I believe God's wisdom and design trumps man's inventiveness one-hundred-fold. Instead of viewing nursing as restrictive, we should view it as God's gracious way of reminding us that nothing else is more important than time with our baby.

I've also observed a mom at work in my second-oldest daughter. In talking with Bethany on the phone in Virginia, we are constantly interrupted by the interactions with her two little sons. Leon, the oldest, is a talker. As a result, Bethany responds to his comments and questions all day long—even as we talk on the phone. She also gives loving words of feedback to little Solomon. Without a doubt, Bethany's ever-present attention is meeting her sons' needs for safety, security, love, and belonging. Bethany and her husband David are doing all they can to raise young men who will be full of confidence and self-esteem.

Our worth as mothers and homemakers is extraordinary. Susanna Wesley (the 25th of 25 children!) impacted the 18th century world through her two sons, revivalists John and Charles Wesley. Her influence through them still resonates today. Of course, her impact came, not by pursuing her own agenda and dreams, but by prioritizing her children. She almost single-handedly raised and educated the 10 of her 19 children who survived infancy. (Her husband was an alcoholic and frequently absent.)[72]

Susanna Wesley's life stands in stark contrast to many Old Testament parents who sacrificed their children for their own success. One example is found in 2 Kings 3:26-27: *When the king of Moab saw that the battle was too fierce for him...he took his oldest son who was to reign in his place, and offered him as a burnt offering on the wall.* God's Word calls us to turn the chief part of our hearts toward our children. Doing so requires that we reject the world's pursuit of self-fulfillment that so often demands the sacrifice of children on altars of personal ambition and success. One path brings life and a blessing. The other brings death and a curse. It all comes down to our priorities.

Mother, oh mother, come shake out your cloth!
Empty the dustpan, poison the moth,
Hang out the washing and butter the bread,
Sew on a button and make up a bed.
Where is the mother whose house is so shocking?
She's up in the nursery, blissfully rocking!

Oh, I've grown as shiftless as Little Boy Blue.
Dishes are waiting and bills are past due.
The shopping's not done, there's nothing for stew,

And out in the yard there's a hullabaloo.
But I'm playing Kanga and this is my Roo.
Look! Aren't her eyes the most wonderful hue?

Oh, cleaning and scrubbing will wait till tomorrow,
But children grow up, as I've learned to my sorrow.
So, quiet down, cobwebs. Dust, go to sleep.
I'm rocking my baby. Babies don't keep.

Ruth Hulburt Hamilton (1958)

Questions for personal use or group discussion:

8. Do you agree with the author's statement that mothers and homemakers are history-makers and world-changers? Explain.

9. How did this chapter on a mother's influence on revival and reformation affect your views on the topic?

10. In what ways is your heart already turned toward your children? In what ways do you think you could improve?

11. Referring to Maslow's Hierarchy of Needs Theory, what needs in your own life were not met as a child? What effect has that had on your life?

12. How did Ruth Hamilton's poem speak to you? Explain.

13. Evaluate and discuss the following quote: *Christian mothers carry their children in hostile territory. When you are in public with them, you are standing with, and defending, the objects of cultural dislike. You are publicly testifying that you value what God values, and that you refuse to value what the world values…You represent everything that our culture hates, because you represent laying down your life for another—and laying down your life for another represents the Gospel.*

Conclusion

A Confident Answer

So, the next time someone asks, "What do you do?" you could answer this way: "Thank you so much for asking! Some would say, 'I'm *just* a mom.' But, I know I am so much more than that. As a mother and homemaker, I hold a position of God-given authority and dominion that has significant impact on the world and history. I directly influence the main building block of society—the family. I also train and mold the leaders of the next generation. The very strength and health of society depends on my faithful diligence. If someone offered me a million dollars to do something else, I would not accept it. I know my job has extraordinary worth and an eternal reward far surpassing anything here on earth."

Endnotes

1   Jankovic, Rachel. "Motherhood is a Calling." 14 July 2011, <http://www.desiringgod.org/blog/posts/motherhood-is-a-calling-and-where-your-children-rank> (accessed 17 June 2013).

2   "Lilac Festival Court." 23 January 2013, <www.spokesman.com/picture-stories/2013-lilac-festival-court/> (accessed 5 April 2013).

3   Rodriguez, Andres. "Youth Ministry's Family Blind Spot." 3 July 2013, <http://www.christianitytoday.com/women/2013/june/youth-ministrys-family-blind-spot.html> (accessed 8 July 2013).

4   Jankovic, Rachel. "Motherhood is a Calling." 14 July 2011, <http://www.desiringgod.org/blog/posts/motherhood-is-a-calling-and-where-your-children-rank> (accessed 17 June 2013).

5   Nappi, Rebecca. "Comstock Friends Reunite." *Spokesman Review*, 10 July 2011.

6   Dannenfelser, Marjorie. "Mothers are our First Home." <http://articlesforheartmindandsoulblogpot.com/2010/05/mothers-are-our-first-home.html> (accessed 24 April 2013).

7   <http://answers.yahoo.com/question/index?qid=20090505125204AAG1iur> (accessed 8 April 2013).

8   < http://www.saveasnowman.org/SAS/HumanImpact/Docs/Forest.html> (accessed 8 April 2013).

9   Rives, Karin. "Trees Help Us Breathe." 24 May 2011, <http://iipdigital.usembassy.gov/st/english/article/2011/05/20110

524121919nirak0.5654718.html#axzz2SNT488uu> (accessed 4 May 2013).

10   Jankovic, Rachel. "Motherhood is a Calling." 14 July 2011, <http://www.desiringgod.org/blog/posts/motherhood-is-a-calling-and-where-your-children-rank> (accessed 17 June 2013).

11   Miss Manners. *The Washington Post.* 5 March 2012,,<http://articles.washingtonpost.com/2012-03-05/lifestyle/35447068_1_balance-work-dreams-mother> (accessed 5 June 2013).

12   Lewis, Katherine. "What are the Mommy Wars?" <http://workingmoms.about.com/od/todaysworkingmoms/f/What-Are-The-Mommy-Wars.htm> (accessed 5 June 2013).

13   Haystack Bible Commentary, god21projectorg, <https://hbiblecommentary.wordpress.com> (accessed 2012)

14   "Reclaiming the 7 Mountains of Influence," <http://www.reclaim7mountains.com/> (accessed 2 April 2013).

15   Archer, Jules. *Breaking Barriers: The Feminist Revolution.* Diane Pub, 1991, p. 41-42.

16   Ward, Geoffrey and Ken Burns. *Not for Ourselves Alone: The Story of Elizabeth Cady Stanton and Susan B. Anthony.* Knopf, 1999, p. 22.

17   Ward and Burns, p. 9.

18   Ward and Burns, p. 20.

19   Ward and Burns, p. 16.

20   Archer, p.86.

21   Friedan, Betty. *Life so Far: A Memoir.* New York: Simon & Schuster, 2006, p. 308.

22   "Humanist Manifesto II." <en.wikipedia.org/wiki/Humanist_Manifesto_II> (accessed 2 May 2013).

23   "Betty Friedan," <en.wikipedia.org/wiki/Betty_Friedan> (accessed 2 May 2013).

24   Wiker, Benjamin. *10 books that Screwed up the World (and 5 other that didn't help).* Washington, DC: Regnery Pub, p.224.

25   Friedan, Betty. *Feminine Mystique*. New York: Norton, 2001, p. 78.

26   *Feminine Mystique*, p. 112.

27   *Life so Far*, p. 163.

28   *Life so Far*, p. 201.

29   *Life so Far*, p. 195-6, 213.

30   *Life so Far*, p. 196.

31   Parker, Kathleen. "Women Find Success, Not Happiness." *Spokesman Review*, 9 June 2013.

32   "The American Family in World War II." <www.u-s-history. com/pages/h1692.html> (accessed 2 April 2013)

33   Hunter, Brenda. *The Power of Mother Love*. Colorado: Waterbrook, 1999, p. 242.

34   "High Clicks." *Vogue*. June 2010, p.160.

35   Slaughter, Anne-Marie. "Why Women Still Can't Have it All," July 2012. *The Atlantic Monthly,* <http//theatlantic.com/magazine/ archive/2012/07/why-women-still-cant-have-it-all/309020/> (accessed 2 April 2013).

36   Slaughter, p. 2.

37   Meir, Golda. <www.scribd.com/doc/233250171/Golda-Meir > p. 3 (accessed 2 April 2013).

38   Meir, Golda, <www.miriamscup.com/meirbiog.htm> (accessed 2 April, 2013).

39   Brawarsky, Sandee. *"Golda Revisted."* <http://www.jwi.org/ page.aspx?pid=726> (accessed 2 April 2013).

40   Pierce, Andrew. "Sad Demise of an Iron Lady." 31 December 2011, <http://www.dailymail.co.uk/news/article-2080536/The-Iron-Lady-Margaret-Thatcher-ignored-children-Christmas.html> (accessed 4 April 2013).

41   Kersten, Katherine. "Does Greater Equality Mean Less Happiness?" 5 October 2009, Star Tribune <http://www.startribune. com/opinion/63332402.html> (accessed 16 July 2013).

42   "The Family in Crisis," Focus on the Family, August, 2001, p.4.

43   Parker, Kathleen. "Women Find Success, Not Happiness." *Spokesman Review*, 9 June 2013.

44   Hess, Bob and Jan. *Full Quiver*. Hess, 1990, p. 126.

45   *English Standard Version Study Bible*. Crossway, 2008, p.56.

46   Webster's 1828 Dictionary

47   Jankovic, Rachel. "Motherhood is a Calling." 14 July 2011, <http://www.desiringgod.org/blog/posts/motherhood-is-a-calling-and-where-your-children-rank> (accessed 17 June 2013).

48   SandRat. "Tomb of the Unknown Soldier" (interesting facts). < http://www.freerepublic.com/focus/f-vetscor/1126293/posts> April, 28, 2004, (accessed 2 April 2013)

49   Bouma, Mary LaGrand. *The Creative Homemaker*, Bethany Fellowship, 1973, p. 169.

50   Jankovic, Rachel. "Motherhood is a Calling." 14 July 2011. <http://www.desiringgod.org/blog/posts/motherhood-is-a-calling-and-where-your-children-rank> (accessed 17 June 2013).

51   "Barefoot and Pregnant." 3 March 2013,.<"http://en.wikipedia.org/wiki/Barefoot_and_pregnant> (accessed 2 April 2013).

52   *ESV Study Bible,* p. 2332.

53   Jankovic, Rachel. "Motherhood is a Calling." <http://www.desiringgod.org/blog/posts/motherhood-is-a-calling-and-where-your-children-rank> (accessed 17 June 2013).

54   Anderson, Lisa. *Are All Those Children Yours?* Anderson, p. 42.

55   "86 Year Old Female Body Builder." <http://forums.sherdog.com/forums/f48/86-yr-old-female-bodybuilder-579631/> (accessed 19 April 2013).

56   Cheaney, Janie. "The Use of a Baby." 15 June 2013. *World Magazine*, p. 26.

57   Sandvig, Zoe. "Far too Few." <http://www.worldmag.com/2008/11/far_too_few> (accessed 27 May 2013).

58   "Day of Conception." <http://en.wikipedia.org/wiki/Day_of_Conception> (accessed 5 July 2013).

59   Hess, Rick and Jan. *A Full Quiver*. 1990, p.14.

60   Hess, p 15-17.

61   Hess, p. 18-20.

62   "The Buzz—Quotables." *World*, 20 January 2007.

63   Taylor, Betsy. "Child Raising Dents Wallet." *The Spokesman Review*, 5 August 2009.

64   Thomas, Oliver. "Might Our Religion be Killing Us?" *USA Today*, 21 April 2008.

65   Hess, p.54-56.

66   Norris, Kathleen. *Mother*. Bulverde: Vision Forum, 1911(reprinted 2000), p.198-199.

67   Norris, p. 184-185.

68   Jankovic, Rachel. "Motherhood is a Calling." 14 July 2011. <http://www.desiringgod.org/blog/posts/motherhood-is-a-calling-and-where-your-children-rank> (accessed 17 June 2013).

69   Olasky, Marvin. "Excellent, Not Elite." <http://www.worldmag.com/2011/03/excellent_not_elite> (accessed 29 May 2013).

70   Webster's 1828 Dictionary

71   "Maslow's Hierarchy of Needs." <http://en.wikipedia.org/wiki/Maslow's_hierarchy_of_needs> (accessed 7 May 2013).

72   "Susanna Wesley." <http://en.wikipedia.org/wiki/Susanna_Wesley> (accessed 22 May 2013).

Additional resources available from Lifeline Ministries

Books

Are All Those Children Yours? by Lisa Anderson
The Heart of a Woman by Jim Anderson
Unmasked: Exposing the Cultural Sexual Assault by Jim Anderson

Messages by Jim Anderson

Identity Theft: The war over the sexual identity of a generation
Authentic Manhood: Breaking the sound barrier
Three Men, Three Destinies: Dealing with sexual temptation
Esther: Discovering the source of true beauty
Protecting our Sons and Daughters
Unmasked conference: A generation's conference on sexuality and relationships

Ordering information and additional resources may be found at www.lifeline-ministries.org